DORLING KINDERSLEY DK EYEWITNESS GUIDES

WORLD WAR II

BRITISH RED CROSS

One-man submarine

Star of
David badge

National emblem
of Hitler's Germany

US
Strategic
Air Forces
sleeve badge

A child's "Mickey
Mouse" gas mask

Japanese
naval
sextant

Symbol of the
Vichy State of
France, 1940–44

British 25-pounder gun

Polish medal

DK EYEWITNESS GUIDES

WORLD WAR II

Russian medal

Written by
SIMON ADAMS

Photographed by
ANDY CRAWFORD

DK

A Dorling Kindersley Book

IN ASSOCIATION WITH
THE IMPERIAL WAR MUSEUM

Beretta pistol
owned by the
Italian viceroy
of Ethiopia

Air raid rattle

Dorling **DK** Kindersley

LONDON, NEW YORK, SYDNEY, DELHI, PARIS,
MUNICH and JOHANNESBURG

Project editor Melanie Halton
Senior art editor Jane Tetzlaff
Art editor Ann Cannings
Assistant editor Jayne Miller
Managing editor Sue Grabham
Senior managing art editor Julia Harris
Additional photography Steve Gorton
Production Kate Oliver
Picture research Mollie Gillard
Senior DTP Designer Andrew O'Brien

This Eyewitness ® Guide has been conceived by
Dorling Kindersley Limited and Editions Gallimard

First published in Great Britain in 2000
by Dorling Kindersley Limited,
80 Strand, London WC2R ORL

4 6 8 10 9 7 5

Copyright © 2000 Dorling Kindersley Limited, London

British fire service badge

A CIP catalogue record for this book is
available from the British Library.

ISBN 0-7513-2876-6

Colour reproduction by
Colourscan, Singapore
Printed in China by
Toppan Printing Co., (Shenzhen) Ltd.

Model of Nazi standard bearer

Straw snow boots made by
German soldiers in Russia

See our complete
catalogue at
www.dk.com

British beach mine

Japanese prayer flag

Contents

Evacuation
card game

A world divided

Hammer

Sickle

SOVIET SYMBOL
The hammer and sickle, seen
on this cap badge, was the
symbol of the Soviet Union
and appeared on the national
flag. The hammer represented
industrial workers, while
the sickle represented peasants
(farm workers).

*Stainless steel figures
are young, strong,
and attractive*

*Worker and
Peasant statue,
made for an
exhibition in
Paris, 1937*

DURING THE EARLY DECADES of the 20th century,
the world was divided into three main political
camps. The first consisted of democratic nations,
where people elected their own governments.
Such countries included Britain, France, the
Low Countries (the Netherlands and Belgium),
Sweden, Czechoslovakia, and the US. The
second – fascist Italy and Spain, Nazi Germany,
nationalist Japan, and the one-party states of
eastern Europe – were ruled by powerful dictators.
The final camp had only one member – the
Soviet Union. This was the world's first
communist state, where the workers were
meant to be in control. But in reality, the
country was run by a tyrannical leader,
Josef Stalin (1879–1953). Conflicts between
the three ideologies concerning territory
and economic wealth led to the world
war that broke out in 1939.

SPREAD OF FASCISM
In 1922, Benito Mussolini
(1883–1945) took power
in Italy and turned the
country into a fascist
(dictator-led) state. By
the 1930s, fascist-style
governments had
taken power in
Spain, Portugal,
Austria, Romania, and in
Germany, where the Nazi
Party took fascist ideas to
their most extreme.

Italian Fascist
Youth march

*Blue-bordered royal
coat of arms*

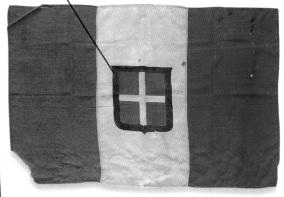

ITALIAN FASCISM
Italian fascists took as their symbol the "fasces" – a
bundle of bound rods that symbolized the power of
Ancient Rome. But throughout Mussolini's time in power,
Italy remained a kingdom under Victor Emmanuel III, and
its official flag (above) showed the royal coat of arms.

Imperial Japanese
army uniform,
c.1930s

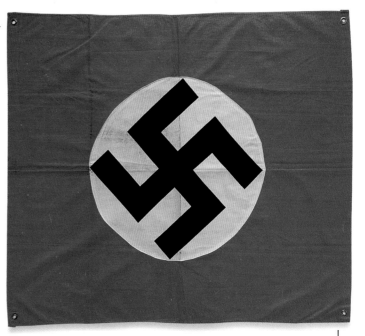
Presentation box for a copy of Mein Kampf

Nazi Party membership book

IMPERIAL JAPAN
During World War I, Japan fought on the side of Britain, France, and the US, but felt cheated by its failure to gain much territory when the peace treaty was drawn up. In the 1920s, the Japanese government came under the increasing control of fanatical nationalists, allied with the army, who wished to make the country a major imperial power in Asia.

HITLER'S PROPOSALS
In 1924, while in prison for trying to seize power in Germany, Hitler wrote *Mein Kampf* (*My Struggle*). The book spelt out Germany's need for a strong leader, a large army, economic self-sufficiency, the suppression of communism, and the extermination of the Jews. Although ignored at the time, the book clearly stated what Hitler intended to do if he won power.

THE NAZI PARTY
Founded in 1920, the National Socialist German Worker's Party, or Nazi Party, was led by Hitler. Nazis believed that German Aryans (white and fair haired) were the master race, and wanted to restore Germany to its former powerful status.

NAZI RALLIES
The Nazis regularly stage-managed vast outdoor rallies, where members paraded with banners and listened to speeches from Hitler and other leading Nazis. When the Nazi Party came to power in Germany in 1933, they held their major rally every year in Nuremberg, south Germany. Such events displayed the strength and determination of the Nazis, as well as the immense power Hitler held over his party.

Nazis stand to attention at the Nuremberg Rally of 1935

Heading to war

In 1933, ADOLF HITLER'S Nazi Party came to power in Germany and began to build up the country's military strength. The Rhineland, a German industrial area which lay next to the border with France and Belgium, had been set as a military-free zone at the end of World War I. Hitler moved his troops back into the Rhineland in 1936, then took over Austria and parts of Czechoslovakia in 1938. Meanwhile, Italy was expanding its power in the Mediterranean and North Africa, and Japan invaded China in 1937. Ties between Germany, Italy, and Japan grew stronger. At first, France and Britain tried to appease the aggressors. However, by the end of the 1930s both countries were re-equipping their armed forces. On the sidelines, the US remained neutral, but watched the rise of Japan in the Pacific Ocean with growing concern. Twenty years after the end of World War I, the world was preparing for war once more.

TREATY OF VERSAILLES
After its defeat in World War I, Germany was forced to sign the Treaty of Versailles in 1919. Germany lost all its overseas empire, as well as land, to its neighbours, and was prevented from maintaining a large army. Most Germans opposed the treaty and supported Hitler's refusal to accept its terms.

EXPLOSIVE EVENTS IN NORTH AFRICA
Italy invaded Ethiopia, then known as Abyssinia, in 1935. The ruler, emperor Haile Selassie (1891-1975), right, was sent into exile. Italy's leader, Mussolini, wanted to build a new Roman Empire in north Africa and turn the Mediterranean into an "Italian lake". Italy also extended its control over Libya and, in 1939, invaded its small neighbour, Albania.

JAPAN INVADES CHINA
After taking over the Chinese province of Manchuria in 1932, Japan embarked on a massive rearmament programme. In 1937, the country launched a full-scale invasion of China, and seized the capital, Nanking, and much of the coast.

DICTATORS TOGETHER
At first, the Italian leader, Mussolini (left), was hostile to Hitler's (right) Nazi Germany. This was because Hitler wanted to take over Austria, Italy's northern neighbour. Gradually, however, the two countries drew closer together. In 1936 they formed a partnership, the Rome–Berlin Axis, which was later extended to include Japan. Italy and Germany later signed a formal alliance, the Pact of Steel, in 1939, and fought together in the early years of the war.

HITLER MOVES INTO AUSTRIA
In March 1938, Hitler took his troops into Austria and declared an *Anschluss*, or union, between the two countries. Hitler had broken the Treaty of Versailles, which banned Germany from uniting with the state. Most Austrians favoured the move, although neighbouring countries were concerned at Hitler's growing power.

BRITAIN AND FRANCE UNITE
The close links between France and Britain in 1938 were marked by this state visit of King George VI (far left) and Queen Elizabeth to France. Behind the scenes, the two countries watched the growing strength of Germany and Italy with alarm. In 1939, as war looked inevitable, France and Britain agreed to help Poland, Romania, and Greece defend their independence if Germany or Italy attacked.

A PEACEFUL APPROACH
Crowds welcomed British Prime Minister, Neville Chamberlain, to Munich in 1938. In an effort to calm events, European leaders had agreed to placate Hitler. They signed the Munich agreement, which let Germans in the Sudeten border region of Czechoslovakia unite with Germany. The Czechs objected, but Chamberlain said it guaranteed "peace for our time". Six months later, Hitler took over the rest of Czechoslovakia.

INVASION OF POLAND
Ready to attack, German forces are seen dismantling Polish border posts in 1939. Hitler had demanded that Poland give up the Polish Corridor – a thin strip of Poland that divided East Prussia from the rest of Germany. Poland resisted, so, on 1 September, he took it. Britain and France had guaranteed to come to Poland's aid if it was invaded. They duly declared war on Germany on 3 September. World War II had begun.

Preparing for the worst

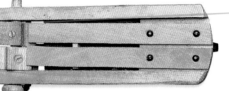

PORTABLE WARNING
Wooden rattles, originally designed to scare birds away from crops, were issued to patrol members of the British Air Raid Precautions (ARP). Designed to warn of potential gas attacks, their loud noise was useful to alert people to enter their air-raid shelters.

As WAR LOOMED between 1938 and 1939, Britain, France, Germany, and Italy began to prepare for the worst. They made plans to ration food and vital raw materials. France had already installed the Maginot Line, built (1929–34) to defend against German invasion. The British government expected London and other cities to be heavily bombed within hours of war starting, so great precautions were taken to protect the civilian population. Shelters were dug in parks and city streets, and gas masks were issued. Plans were drawn up to evacuate thousands of children from the cities to the countryside. The outbreak of war in September 1939 brought many of these plans into operation, but it was not until the German invasion of Scandinavia, the Low Countries, and France, in April and May of 1940, that many of the preparations were tested for the first time.

GUARDING THE HOME FRONT
Towards the end of the war, German men aged 16 to 60, who were not already in the army, were called to the Volkssturm (home guard). Like the British Home Guard, set up in May 1940, they had few uniforms and little training, and had to make do with whatever weapons they could lay their hands on.

Troops and weapons are transported on the Maginot underground railway

FRENCH DEFENCE
The main defensive fortification in France was the Maginot Line. It took five years to construct and stretched along France's eastern border with Germany, from Luxembourg in the north to Switzerland in the south. The line consisted of anti-tank defences, bomb-proof artillery shelters, and strengthened forts, many of which were linked by underground railways.

Tin-can mortar bomb

Grenade made from a wine bottle

IMPROVISED WEAPONS
The British Home Guard had few weapons and often had to improvise. They used cans to make mortar bombs and bottles to make petrol bombs and grenades. The Home Guard was a volunteer organization, set up to protect vital defence installations, and watch out for any enemy infiltration.

German gas mask

GAS MASKS
In Britain everyone was issued with a gas mask. In Germany, however, only those considered high risk, such as children, air-raid wardens, and Nazi Party officials were given masks. Since gas was never used by either side, the masks were never actually needed.

Gas filter

S.Filtereinsatz für den zivilen Luftschu
...et gegen alle chemischen Kampfstoffe sowie gegen saure Ga...
...gegen Schwebstoffe (Nebel und Rauche)   Schützt nicht geg...

Der Feind sieht Dein Licht!

Verdunkeln!

BLACKOUT PRECAUTIONS
"The enemy sees your light! Make it dark!" This German poster warns civilians to obey the blackout by keeping all lights shielded at night or risk helping enemy bombers to find their town. From the outbreak of the war, blackouts were compulsory throughout Germany and Britain.

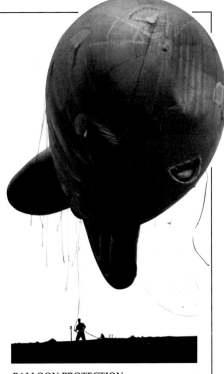

BALLOON PROTECTION
Large, inflatable barrage balloons protected the major towns and cities of Britain from air raids. These balloons were launched before a raid and trailed a network of steel cables beneath them. Incoming bombers had to fly high to avoid becoming entangled with the cables, thereby reducing their accuracy.

AIR-RAID SHELTERS
Most British city-dwellers with a garden installed an Anderson shelter to provide protection during air raids. The Anderson, a corrugated-iron tunnel, was usually sunk in the ground and covered with earth. In February 1941, Morrison shelters (steel cages for use indoors) were introduced for those without gardens.

German civilian ration card

RESOURCE RATIONING
Food and petrol were rationed in Germany from the outset of war. For many poorer Germans, subsidised food offered a more varied and therefore healthier diet than before the war. It was only in 1943 that rationing became severe.

BEACH DEFENCE
Mines were planted on possible invasion beaches in southern Britain and northern France. The mines were designed to inflict maximum damage on any invasion force.

British beach mine

Lightning attack

German foreign minister *Joachim von Ribbentrop*

Russian foreign minister *Vyacheslav Molotov*

Soviet leader Josef Stalin

NAZI-SOVIET PACT
On 23 August 1939, the foreign ministers of Russia and Germany signed a non-aggression pact in Moscow. The pact allowed Germany to invade Poland and western Europe without fear of a Russian attack. They met again afterwards, on 28 September, pictured here, to confirm their division of Poland between them.

"Blitzkrieg", the German word for lightning war, was a military technique used to great effect by Germany during the war. Highly mobile Panzer (armoured) forces blasted their way into enemy territory ahead of the slower-moving infantry, who followed behind to mop up all resistance. Such was the speed and ferocity of these attacks that they often caught their enemies unawares. When Blitzkrieg attacks overwhelmed Poland, in September 1939, Britain and France declared war on Germany. Between May and June 1940, Germany overpowered France and the Low Countries. Yet, in Western Europe the Germans had fewer tanks and troops than the combined forces of Britain, France and Belgium. They did, however, have air superiority. Skilful planning, rapid attacks, and concentrated firepower saw Germany triumph in the west by June 1940.

British newspaper announces the start of World War II

Dropping bomb

WAR DECLARED
Britain and France declared war against Germany on 3 September 1939. This meant their vast overseas empires were at war as well. Most European countries, however, including Ireland, Switzerland, Spain, and Portugal, together with the US, remained neutral.

MOTORBIKE ADVANCE
German mechanized Panzer units used motorbikes with sidecars to drive fast into enemy territory. Their swift arrival ahead of the main army often surprised the enemy and led to considerable success.

PANZER ATTACK
The main power behind the Blitzkrieg came from the tank units (portrayed here in the film, *Blitzkrieg*), supported from the air by bombers. Their advance was so quick and efficient in destroying enemy positions that Panzer units often had to wait for the infantry to catch up.

DIVE BOMBERS

The Junkers Ju87 (Stuka) dive bomber was the main attacking aircraft used during the Blitzkrieg. The Stukas were fitted with sirens which sounded like screaming as they dived almost vertically out of the sky to drop their bombs on a terrified population.

THROWING WEAPONS

Hand and stick grenades were used by the German infantry as they advanced into enemy territory. Grenades were thrown to kill enemy troops and clear buildings of snipers.

Hand grenade

Stick grenade

TAKING FRANCE

The devastion caused to northern France can be seen in this photograph of Calais after a Blitzkrieg bombing raid. Such rapid destruction led to the collapse of France within six weeks and the defeat of the French army.

STORMING THE LOW COUNTRIES

In May 1940, heavily armed German troops poured over the border into Belgium, Luxembourg, and the Netherlands. The Dutch flooded much of their own country so as to slow the advance. Their forces were no match, however, for the German army and they surrendered after four days. Belgium and Luxembourg followed soon after.

Stick grenade is tucked into boot so it can be drawn quickly

Occupation

ACROSS EUROPE, PEOPLE REACTED differently to life under German occupation. Some joined the resistance (trying to undermine German plans) or refused to co-operate with their occupiers. Others actively collaborated with the Germans, welcoming them as defenders against communism and supporting their anti-Jewish policies. For most people, however, there was little choice but to passively accept the situation. In France and Norway, the governments actively collaborated with Germany. The name of the pro-German leader in Norway, Vidkun Quisling, has entered the language as a word for traitor. But the pre-war leaders of Poland, Czechoslovakia, Norway, the Netherlands, Luxembourg, Greece, and Yugoslavia all fled to London. Once there, they set up governments in exile. King Leopold of Belgium remained as a prisoner, and the Danish king, Christian X, and his government stayed in Denmark, collaborating little. The real power always lay with the occupying Germans.

Ear piece

Plaque of the LVF

BROTHERS IN ARMS
The French Légion de Volontaires Français (LVF) was a fiercely anti-communist organization. The LVF raised volunteers to fight alongside the Germans on the eastern front against Soviet Russia.

Hitler visits Paris nine days after the Nazis took control

HITLER IN PARIS
German troops entered an undefended Paris on 14 June 1940, after a campaign that had lasted little more than a month. Two million citizens managed to flee the city in advance. Once the shock of occupation was over, however, life continued much as before, with German officers mixing with the locals.

Home-made wireless receiver used by a Dutch family during the occupation

SECRET RADIO
Hidden in a tin, this radio was used by a Dutch family to listen to the BBC (British Broadcasting Corporation). Broadcasts included general war news, messages from the exiled Dutch royals, and coded messages to secret agents. Owning a radio was forbidden in many occupied countries, but that did not stop people from making their own and using them in secret.

A French collaborator has her hair cropped

THE COLLABORATORS
Throughout occupied Europe, many people actively collaborated with the Germans. Some betrayed their neighbours for supporting the resistance, others passed on information. A few women even lived with German officers. As their countries were liberated, some locals took revenge against the collaborators by beating or shooting them, or by shaving the women's heads.

Lapel badge bearing the Vichy State double-headed axe

NEW SYMBOLS

During the rule of the Vichy goverment, many symbols of Republican France were replaced by Vichy symbols. These included the double-headed axe and, most commonly, portraits of Marshal Pétain.

English cross of St George

OPERATION DYNAMO

Between 26 May and 4 June 1940, 338,226 soldiers were evacuated from the French beaches of Dunkirk during Operation Dynamo. As the German army sped through northern France towards the English Channel, they trapped the British and much of the French army. A fleet of British, French, Dutch, and Belgian ships sailed backwards and forwards across the Channel to rescue the soldiers. All equipment was left behind. The battle of France was a huge defeat for the British army, but the successful evacuation did much to raise morale at a dangerous time.

VICHY FRANCE

French leader Marshal Pétain agreed to an armistice with Germany on 21 June, 1940. France had to accept German occupation in the north and west. Pétain headed a puppet state (supposedly independent but actually controlled by Germany) from the southern town of Vichy. The Vichy government collaborated with the Germans, deporting Jews and providing many vital supplies. In November 1942 the Germans took up occupation and the state eventually collapsed in August 1944.

TO THE RESCUE

At only 4.4 m (14 ft) long, *Tamzine* was the smallest vessel to take part in Operation Dynamo (see above). It was one of more than 900 boats that ranged from minesweepers and destroyers to privately owned pleasure craft and fishing boats. *Tamzine* ferried many men from the beach to deep-water vessels before being towed back to England by a Belgian trawler.

Tamzine, the smallest civilian vessel to cross the channel during Operation Dynamo

SHOWING SUPPORT
Resistance groups often wore identifying armbands, such as this one from the Polish Home Army. The group was formed in 1942 to fight the occupying German army. It led the Warsaw uprising in August 1944, but was crushed by the Germans.

THE COLOUR OF FREEDOM
Dutch resistance groups were very effective in Europe. Members provided support and shelter for persecuted Jews, and gave valuable assistance to Allied pilots and airborne troops.

FREE FRENCH FORCES
When France fell to the Germans, General Charles de Gaulle fled to London. He broadcast an appeal, on 18 June 1940, for people to join the fight for Free France.

SPYING ON THE ENEMY
Danish resistance to German occupation grew as conditions in the country worsened. By 1943, a large movement was spying for Britain and carrying out strikes and acts of sabotage.

Resistance

AT FIRST, THE RESPONSE of the people of Europe to the invasion and occupation of their homelands was unco-ordinated and ineffectual. Armed resistance was scattered and it was left to heroic individuals to risk their lives to help Allied servicemen escape, or give shelter to persecuted Jews. Gradually organized groups began to gain ground, supported with arms and intelligence from Britain, while Communist groups in Eastern Europe received some help from Russia after 1941. As the Germans became harsher, using slave labour and rounding up Jews, Slavs, and other peoples they considered "subhuman", it led to increasing resistance across the continent. By the time liberation came in 1944–45, partisan groups were fighting alongside the invading British, American, and Russian forces.

KING CHRISTIAN X
When Germany invaded Denmark on 9 April 1940, King Christian X (1870–1949) stayed put, unlike the monarchs of most other occupied countries. The Danish government avoided co-operating with Germany when possible, and even helped most of the country's 8,000 Jews to escape to neutral Sweden.

Genuine stamp

Fake stamp

Resistance stamps show a larger bag under the left eye

SPOT THE DIFFERENCE
Communicating by post was a risky business for resistance groups. The Germans intercepted and forged letters sent by the French Resistance leading to the discovery and death of members. To make sure they knew which letters to trust, fake French stamps were printed by the British intelligence, changing one tiny detail.

French ration card, driving licence, and army paper

Yeo-Thomas's fake identity card – he had to perfect a new signature as François Tirelli

SECRET LIVES
Undercover agents took on new identities backed up by forged documents. British agent Forest Frederick Edward Yeo-Thomas (1901-64), known as "White Rabbit", worked with the French Resistance on three missions. He became François Thierry, then Tirelli, born in Algiers. He was caught in 1944 and tortured by the Gestapo, but survived.

Skeleton butt – a lightweight frame

Trigger

RESISTANCE-MADE GUNS
The British Sten sub-machine gun was light and simple to use. It could be produced easily and cheaply, and was copied by resistance groups in occupied Europe who manufactured their own versions. The 9 mm Mark II shown here was built by members of the Danish resistance.

ATTACKING FROM THE BUSHES
A commander of a French Maquis resistance group briefs fighters before a raid. French resistance to German occupation began as soon as the German armies entered France in May 1940, but was largely ineffectual. By 1941, a small number of organized armed resistance groups were in operation. They became known as the Maquis, a Corsican term for bush or scrub, as they hid in the undergrowth then sprung out to fight invaders.

UP THEIR SLEEVES
The Free French forces used small knives hidden in their lapels or up their sleeves to attack their captors and escape. The results were often messy, but effective. The badge of the Free French – the Cross of Lorraine – can be seen on the knife's sheath.

A sheath is attached to an armband worn under clothes

BRAVE WIDOW
Violette Szabo (1921–45) sold perfume in London, before joining the Special Operations Executive (SOE). She joined after her husband was killed fighting for the Free French army. Szabo was twice dropped into France, the last time in June 1944, to help a resistance group. She was captured and died in a concentration camp.

Silencer eliminates most of the sound of the blast

P.BERETTA-CAL.9 SCURT-Mº 1934-BREVE T.
GARDONE V.T-1941

SILENT WEAPONS
This silenced 9 mm Beretta pistol was used by agents of the Italian Organizzazione di Vigilanza e Repressione dell'Antifascismo (OVRA). The group, set up to suppress opposition to Italian Fascism, fought resistance groups in the French Alps and in the Balkans.

TITO'S PARTISANS
The most successful European resistance group were the Yugoslav Partisans, seen here in combat training. The army was organized by the Communist Party leader Tito (1892–1980) and grew to 150,000 members. In 1944, a combined Partisan and Russian Red Army force regained the Yugoslav capital, then the whole country, from German occupiers.

In the German army

THE GERMAN ARMED SERVICES were not one single fighting force but a tangle of different organizations. Each one reported separately to Hitler as Commander-in-Chief. The Wehrmacht was the main army, and was entirely distinct from the Schutzstaffel (SS), which Hitler introduced to support his National Socialist Party. Many members of the secret police (Gestapo) held SS rank. The armed Panzer (tank) divisions, the navy (Kriegsmarine), and the air force (Luftwaffe) were also separate, as were the reserve forces, the various militias, and the Brownshirts. Uniforms and emblems were important to create a strong identity and an image that would attract a young, loyal force. The armed services were well equipped, at times very well organized, and until late 1942, regarded by many as invincible.

Death's head emblem

Field cap

DRESSED TO KILL
SS Panzer troop members wore a black, close-fitting, short jacket (*panzerjacke*) well suited to the cramped conditions inside a tank. Their field cap was decorated with both the national German emblem and the SS death's head.

Divisional badge

Collar patch with victory runes, or symbols

SS Panzer jacket

Division title "Adolf Hitler"

Belt

SS motto "Meine Ehre heisst Treue" (Loyalty is my honour)

Trousers

Belt webbing

HEAVY ARMOUR
German tank troops belonged to the Panzer army. Panzer is the German word for armour. The PzKpfw IV (right) was one of 2,500 tanks that rolled into France in 1940, as 10 panzer divisions invaded.

WORN WITH PRIDE
This silver on black badge showing the national emblem was worn by the Waffen-SS, the combat divisions of the SS. At its peak in 1942–43, the Waffen-SS had 39 divisions with more than 900,000 soldiers.

Eagle

Swastika – an ancient symbol for good luck

National emblem

Edging

Ankle slit

Boots

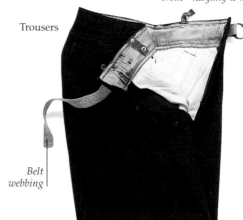

HIDDEN HORRORS
One of the most widely used anti-tank guns in the German army was the Pak 38 (left). It was the only gun able to tackle the well-armoured and all-but invincible Soviet T34 tanks. It had a range of 2,750 m (9,023 ft) while its low silhouette meant that it could be hidden from enemy vision.

Loops to tow gun

Solid wheels reduced need for maintenance

General officer's cap

Rank badge for Major General

Oak and laurel leaves

Gold oak-leaf collar patch for general officer

National emblem

SERVING IN STYLE
Hitler's new national emblem – a swastika clutched by an eagle – was added to all standard German army uniforms. He did, however, keep much of the traditional army insignia, such as badges showing rank. Different coloured piping identified each branch of the army – crimson for the general staff, white for infantry, and red for artillery.

Ribbon bar

Iron cross 1st Class, 1939

Hook for dagger

Division title "Grossdeutschland" (Greater Germany)

Field service tunic

Belt with holster

Holster

General officer's breeches

Fob watch pocket

Broad red stripe indicates the wearer was a general officer in the artillery unit

Calf laces tighten the bottom of the breeches

General officer's boots

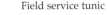

Rocket

MOANING MINNIE
The nebelwerfer (fog thrower) was capable of firing 32-kg (70-lb) rockets up to 6,900 m (22,639 ft). Its location was easily detected as a rocket threw out a 12-m (40-ft) brilliant flame as it shot into the air. The British nicknamed the launcher "Moaning Minnie" on account of the noise it made as it fired.

BROWNSHIRTS
Soldiers in the Sturmabteilung (SA), or storm division, were known as the Brownshirts because of their uniform. Formed in 1921 to protect Nazi speakers at public meetings, the force grew to more than 500,000. Following a power struggle between the SA and the army, however, their powers were greatly reduced in June 1934.

SS ARMBAND
This distinctive armband was worn by members of the Schutzstaffel (SS), the most feared organization in Nazi Germany. Renowned for violence and cruelty, the SS was also responsible for running the concentration camps.

LOOKING THE PART
The Schutzstaffel, or SS, seen here on parade, was originally created by Hitler as his personal bodyguard. Its head, Heinrich Himmler, turned it into a separate security force within the Nazi state. With their grey coats and death's head cap badges, the Schutzstaffel were responsible for many of the worst Nazi crimes.

ON THE BATTLE LINE
A German infantry man pauses in front of a burning Russian farm. He was one of 12.5 million soldiers who served in the German army during the course of the war. The infantry (foot soldiers) played a major role, fighting all the way to the outskirts of Moscow before retreating to defend Berlin.

The Battle of Britain

WITH THE FALL OF FRANCE IN JUNE 1940, Hitler hoped that Britain might settle for peace. Britain, however, under its new leader Winston Churchill, had no intention of doing so. Thus, Hitler decided to launch a huge seaborne invasion – Operation Sea Lion – across the English Channel. For this to work, the German air force (Luftwaffe) had to defeat the British Royal Air Force (RAF). The first attack on British airfields commenced on 10 July 1940. Waves of German Dornier bombers flew over southeast England escorted by Messerschmitt fighters. British Hurricanes and Spitfires took to the skies in retaliation. Day after day, battles raged across the sky. The RAF gradually won control and in October 1940 Germany stopped the operation.

Eight Browning machine guns in leading edges of wings

SPITFIRE
At the outset of the war, the Spitfire Mk 1A was the RAF's most modern fighter. Capable of speeds up to 582 kph (362 mph), it was faster at high altitudes and far more manoeuvrable than its German rival, the Messerschmitt Bf109E.

INTERNATIONAL AIR FORCE
The RAF had pilots from all around the world, including Poles, Czechoslavs, and Frenchmen, who had fled their German-occupied countries. There were also many Canadians and New Zealanders, as well as seven Americans, although the US was not yet at war. New pilots received a maximum of only 10 hours' training before being sent up to fight.

Two RAF navigators (left) study a map with their Polish pilots

Mobile anti-aircraft radar receiver

ENEMY DETECTION
Radar was hugely important to the RAF's success because it alerted them to incoming enemy aircraft. Radar systems used 90-m (300-ft) steel masts to emit radio signals. The signals bounced off enemy planes and were picked up by radar receivers. This alerted pilots to scramble into the air to resume battle.

FIGHTING LIKE DOGS
As the RAF and the Luftwaffe fought for control of the skies, dogfights (close-up battles between fighter aircraft) were common. Such fights, portrayed here in the film *Battle of Britain*, often required huge bravery from young, under-trained and exhausted pilots.

> *"Never in the field of human conflict was so much owed by so many to so few."*
>
> WINSTON CHURCHHILL

Bf110C Messerschmitts

MESSERSCHMITTS
Two types of Messerschmitts formed the mainstay of the Luftwaffe fighter force. The Bf110C was an escort fighter for long-range bombers. Slow and hard to handle, however, it was no match for the British Hurricanes and Spitfires. The Bf110C's faster partner, the Bf109E, was superior to the Hurricane, but its range of 660 km (410 miles) limited its effectiveness.

Twin fins on tail

GÖRING'S AIR FORCE
Chief of the Luftwaffe, Reichsmarschall Hermann Göring, and his officers watched the Battle of Britain from the French coast. Göring believed the Luftwaffe could destroy air defences in southern England within four days and the RAF in four weeks. This, he hoped, would enable Germany to take over Britain. The Luftwaffe, however, failed to achieve victory.

ON WATCH
Ground crew used powerful and sturdy binoculars to keep a lookout for enemy aircraft. These ones were used by the Luftwaffe on the German home front. Both sides used radar for long-distance observations. In the close-up air battles, combat pilots had to stay continually alert for the movements of enemy aircraft.

Direction finder

Powerful lenses

Luftwaffe observation binoculars

Eye piece

Binoculars rotate for an all-round view of the skies

Bombing raids

British fire service badge

THERE WAS NO MORE TERRIFYING a sound in war than the drone of incoming enemy bomber planes. They were laden with high explosives and incendiary bombs, ready to drop on top of homes and destroy cities. Each side believed that the destruction of strategic installations (oil refineries, factories, and railways) would cripple the enemy war effort. They also hoped that bombing civilian targets would destroy morale and force a surrender. Thus, Britain endured the Blitz from 1940 to 1941, while Germany was bombed repeatedly from 1942, and Japan from 1944. Many thousands of people were killed, houses destroyed, and ancient buildings ruined.

Two Blitz survivors, their home in ruins, peer out from the shelter that saved their lives

AIR-RAID SURVIVAL
During air raids some people hid in underground shelters while others sought refuge in cellars or in makeshift shelters in their own homes. The heavy bombing of European, Japanese, and Chinese cities was devastating, yet many did survive.

BOMB POWER
Late in the war, Germany launched its most secret and deadly weapons. They were the V-1 flying bomb and the V-2 rocket (V stood for vengeance). Both bombs carried 1-tonne warheads and were capable of great damage. Many V-1s, however, were shot out of the skies or missed their targets, since they were difficult to aim accurately.

V-2 was 14 m (46 ft) long, weighed 13 tonnes, and flew at an altitude of 80 km (50 miles)

V-2 rocket

FIRE FIGHTING
Most of the damage done by bombs was caused by the fires that they ignited. Fire fighters risked their lives to keep the flames under control. It was also their duty to make sure that no one was trapped in the burning buildings.

London firemen tackle a blaze in a warehouse, 1941

HOT BOMBS
Thousands of these incendiary bombs were dropped on British and German cities during the war. Filled with combustible chemicals, such as magnesium or phosphorus, the bombs were designed to set buildings alight by creating great heat.

Magnesium incendiary bomb

THE BLITZ
Between September 1940 and May 1941, Germany tried to force Britain to surrender by bombing its major cities. Germany launched 127 large-scale night raids. Seventy-one of these were against London, the rest against cities such as Liverpool, Glasgow, and Belfast. More than 60,000 civilians were killed and 2 million homes were destroyed in what was known as the Blitz.

BOMBS AWAY
Heavy bombers, such as these US Flying Fortresses, carried bomb loads up to 5,800 kg (12,800 lb). Such firepower enabled bombers to do immense damage to both strategic installations and to civilian populations.

Gun sight

BOMBING OF DRESDEN
The Allied bombing raid against the German city of Dresden in February 1945 was one of the most controversial events of the war. The bombs created a firestorm which destroyed every building and killed 30,000 to 60,000 civilians. With few military targets in the city, many people condemned the raid against unarmed civilians as a war crime.

DEFENDING THE PILOT
Being a gunner on a bomber plane was a very precarious job. Gunners sat or stood in exposed gun turrets to give them a clear view of the surrounding skies, and any approaching enemy aircraft.

Dresden still in ruins, two years after the raid

GUNNER AWARD
The German Luftwaffe (air force) awarded its war service badge to gunners on the basis of points. Shooting down an enemy aircraft was worth four points. Four aircraft, or 16 points, were required to receive the award.

BOMBER MACHINE GUN
The only defence carried by a bomber was provided by gunners equipped with powerful machine guns. Once up in the air, the slow-flying and heavily laden bomber was an easy target to enemy fighter planes or to ground attack from anti-aircraft fire. Whenever possible, bombers flew in large convoys escorted by fast, nimble fighter planes to fend off any attack.

Rear machine gun from a Heinkel bomber

A London street after a night of bombing during the Blitz

Air raid wardens and civilians search for survivors among the wreckage of buildings

Total war

Stalin's shoulder strap

U<small>NTIL MID</small>-1941, the war was fought mainly in Europe and North Africa. On one side were the Axis (Germany, Italy, and some east European countries). On the other side were the Allies (Britain, France, and their vast empires). After the fall of France in June 1940, Britain stood alone against the Axis. This situation changed when Germany invaded Russia, and Japan attacked the US at Pearl Harbor and the British in Malaya. The war was then fought on a worldwide scale. Only South America was not involved with actual fighting. Battles raged from the North Atlantic to the Pacific Ocean, and from the deserts of North Africa to the frozen Steppes (grasslands) of Russia, and to the jungles of southeast Asia.

Map showing the extent of Axis contol in Europe

OCCUPIED EUROPE
By November 1942, Germany and Italy occupied most of Europe. Only Britain and Russia were fighting against them. In North Africa, the Allies had occupied Morocco and Algeria and were driving the Germans out of Egypt into Libya.

☐ Axis states

☐ Areas controlled by Axis

☐ Allied states

☐ Areas controlled by Allies

☐ Neutral states

-- Extent of German military occupation

FIGHTING FOR FRANCE
When France was invaded by Germany, General Charles de Gaulle (left) went to Britain and raised the banner of Free France. At first, his support was limited. Eventually, he led a large group of overseas French troops and resistance fighters.

German Panzer units pass through a blazing Russian village, torched by fleeing civilians

INTO RUSSIA
On 22 June 1941, the Germans mounted a surprise attack against Russia. The attack broke the 1939 Nazi-Soviet Pact in which both sides agreed not to fight each other. The invasion – known as Operation Barbarossa – brought Russia into the war on the same side as Britain.

British Prime Minister Winston Churchill (1874–1965)

US President Franklin Roosevelt (1882–1945)

Soviet leader Josef Stalin (1879–1953)

THE BIG THREE
The leaders of Britain, Russia, and the US are pictured here at Yalta in the Crimea, Russia, in February 1945. These three men met twice during the war to decide on strategies for co-ordinating their war effort.

PEARL HARBOR ATTACK
On 7 December 1941, Japan launched a surprise attack on the US naval base of Pearl Harbor in Hawaii. Nineteen ships were destroyed and 2,403 sailors killed. US President Roosevelt called it "a day that will live in infamy". On 8 December, Congress declared war on Japan and Germany.

MUSSOLINI'S ITALY

Mussolini (right) did not bring Italy into the war on Germany's side until June 1940. At this time Italy declared war on Britain and France and invaded southern France. In October 1940, Italy invaded Greece and, in 1941, divided Yugoslavia with Germany. Italian troops also fought with the Germans in Russia, but Italy always remained the junior partner in the Axis.

Hitler and Mussolini drive through Florence, Italy

GENERAL TOJO

Hideki Tojo (1884–1948) led the pro-military party in Japan from 1931, and sided closely with Germany and Italy. He became prime minister in October 1941. Under his rule, Japan attacked US and British territory in Asia, and extended the Japanese empire across southeast Asia and the Pacific Ocean. He was tried for war crimes in 1948, and executed.

General Hideki Tojo on the cover of a Japanese wartime magazine

JAPANESE CONTROL

By early 1942, Japan had overrun the whole of southeast Asia and much of the Pacific Ocean. The US naval victory at Midway, in June 1942, halted the Japanese advance.

▨ Japanese-controlled area by 1942

--- Extent of Japanese expansion

Pearl Harbor under attack

A naval ship explodes during the Japanese bombing

In enemy territory

THROUGHOUT THE WAR, many men and women risked their lives by entering enemy-occupied countries. They went to spy on the invading forces, work with resistance fighters, and carry out acts of sabotage to foil enemy plans. Governments made extensive use of a network of spies. The British set up the Special Operations Executive (SOE) and the Americans, the Office of Strategic Services (OSS), to train agents to work undercover deep in enemy territory. Technicians were kept busy devising ingenious ways to hide radios, maps, and other equipment needed for a successful mission. Not everyone succeeded, and many SOE members were killed or captured, tortured, and sent to concentration camps. Few survived to tell of their remarkable deeds.

SUICIDE PILL
British secret agents carried with them an L-pill (L stands for lethal). This was to be swallowed if the spy was captured by enemy agents. The pill killed in five seconds, too quick for any life-saving measures to take effect. Agents concealed pills in a variety of personal effects, such as lockets, rings and other jewellery.

Tiny compass *Concealed compartment*

PLANS IN THE PIPE-LINER
Perfectly normal-looking from the outside, this pipe contained hidden secrets. The bowl was lined with asbestos so that the pipe could be smoked without setting light to a message or map concealed within. The stem also contained a miniature compass.

Blade *Holes cut for display*

HIDDEN KNIFE
MI9, a British government organization involved in helping prisoners of war escape, designed this pencil to conceal a blade, useful in any escape attempt. A simple pencil would not arouse suspicion during search or interrogation, so may not be confiscated.

End unscrewed to load

Cartridge

SECRET AGENT SORGE
Richard Sorge (1895–1944), seen on a Soviet stamp, was a German journalist who spied for Russia. While working for a newspaper in Japan, he learned that Japan planned to attack Asia in 1941, rather than Russia. This was vital information to Russia, leaving her troops free to fight Germany.

PROPELLING PENCIL PISTOL
By unscrewing the end and inserting a 6.35 mm cartridge, this propelling pencil became a pistol. The casing contained a spring-loaded hammer to fire the cartridge, which was released by a button on the side.

Button pulled back to fire

DANGEROUS DATE
The SOE sent French-born Odette Sansom into southern France in 1942 to link up with a unit working with the Resistance, led by Peter Churchill. Both were captured in 1943 and interrogated by German officers. They survived a concentration camp and married after the war.

POISON PEN THREAT
This needle-firing pen was among the ingenious weapons designed by the British for agents working undercover A sharp gramophone needle could be fired at an enemy by pulling the cap back and releasing it. They were not lethal – the idea was that users would spread a rumour that the needles were poisoned.

Tuning dial

FOOTPRINT DISGUISE
The SOE issued its agents with feet-shaped rubber soles to attach to their boots when landing on a beach. The resulting footprints disguised their bootprints. This confused the Japanese into thinking the prints were from local people walking barefoot on the sand, not from enemy agents.

Straps fastened the rubber sole over agent's boots

Cover with English labels

POCKET RADIO
Abwehr, the German military intelligence, issued its agents with this small battery-powered radio. Agents could transmit and receive Morse code messages while on operations. All labels were written in English so as not to give its user away if captured.

SECRETS UNDERFOOT

Compartments inside the rubber heels of boots made ideal hiding places for messages, maps, and other printed papers. Both sides used this simple invention to great effect during the war. However, it was often the first place the enemy looked when interrogating a suspect.

Message hidden in the heel

MESSAGES FROM A SUITCASE

Suitcase radios were used by both sides to broadcast messages from inside enemy territory. For authenticity, some US radios were concealed in suitcases taken from European refugees who arrived in New York City. Messages were transmitted in Morse code, using a system of sounds in place of letters.

Headphones allowed agents to listen to incoming messages

Plug connected transmitter to mains power

PARACHUTED TO HER DEATH

Not every SOE operation was a great success. Madeleine Damerment was dropped by parachute into occupied France along with two other agents in February 1944. She was captured on landing. After interrogation, she was sent to Dachau concentration camp where she was executed. Many SOE agents met a similar fate.

CARD TRICKS

Hidden inside this playing card is part of an escape map. The map was divided into numbered sections. To piece it together, escapees would have to soak the tops off the rest of the pack and put the sections in order. Then they could plot their route home.

Frequency dial

Spare valve

A FOREIGN MATCH

This matchbox looks French but it was made in Britain for SOE agents. Members working abroad could not take any objects with them that might betray their true identity. All belongings had to look locally made, so they were specially printed.

Top of card peeled off to reveal map

Lens opening

Key used to tap out Morse code

This Mark II radio was used by Oluf Reed Olsen, a Norwegian agent working for Britain in occupied Norway

Crystal plug used to change transmission frequency

Battery clips connected transmitter to car battery for use without mains power

MATCHBOX CAMERA

The Kodak company in the US developed this tiny matchbox camera for use by OSS intelligence agents so they could take pictures without the enemy noticing. The label on the front of the matchbox was changed according to the country in which the camera was used.

The Prisoners

As THE TIDE OF WAR EBBED and flowed, many millions of soldiers were captured or surrendered to enemy forces. In the first three months of the 1941 German invasion of Russia alone, more than 2 million Red Army soldiers were taken prisoner. For most of these prisoners of war (POWs), their fighting days were over, and they were forced to spend months, if not years, locked up in specially built prison camps. International agreements, such as the Geneva Convention of 1929, were meant to guarantee that prisoners were well looked after, but some captors disregarded this. POWs in German camps suffered greatly as their rations were cut in the final months of the war. Many prisoners devised ingenious ways to escape, although few succeeded and the punishments were sometimes severe for those who were caught.

MARKED MEN
All POWs had to carry identification (ID) tags with them at all times. These two came from the Oflag XVIIA and Stalag VI/A camps in Germany.

CAMP CURRENCY
Allied POWs held in German camps were paid with special camp money (*Lagergeld*) for the work they did. The money, such as the 1, 2, and 5 Reichsmark banknotes above, could be used to buy razors, shaving soap, toothpaste, and occasionally extra food rations from the camp canteen.

Polish POWs cook smuggled food on homemade stoves inside their huts at a German prison camp

LIFE IN CAPTIVITY
The Geneva Convention was an international agreement on the human rights of POWs. It stated that they must be clothed, given food and lodgings as good as their guards, allowed to keep possessions, practise their religion and receive medical treatment. The Convention was not always kept, and many prisoners were held in degrading conditions.

BUCKLE BLADE
Some prisoners managed to sneak in simple tools. A blade hidden on a belt buckle could help POWs to cut themselves free if they were tied up.

Miniature saw blade

BUTTON COMPASS
A tiny yet effective compass could be concealed inside a button. Once free, an escapee could use it to navigate across enemy territory to safety.

Compass needle

Pivoting blades

FLYING AWAY
The building of this glider in the attic of Colditz Castle, Germany, was one of many ingenious escape plans. Colditz was a punishment camp for Allied officers who tried to escape from less-secure camps. Of the 1,500 POWs held there, 176 attempted to escape, but only 31 succeeded.

CLEVER GADGETS
Escape blades were nailed to soldiers' metal shoe heels. Sometimes they were fixed onto the sides of coins. It was assumed that prisoners would be allowed to keep loose change, even if the guards took their banknotes.

Nail securing blade to heel

Homemade plane (below) and saw

MEN WITH A MISSION
Prisoners in Colditz and other camps used whatever materials came to hand to help them escape. The basic tools (left), made from bedposts and scraps of metal, were used in Colditz to build the escape glider (above).

Flying boot

ESCAPE BOOT
British RAF pilots wore flying boots that could be easily cut down and converted into civilian shoes. For this, they would use a penknife hidden in a concealed pocket. The idea was to enable airmen forced down in enemy territory to blend in with civilians and avoid capture.

Cut-down shoe

Red Cross food parcel

A RARE TREAT

Under the Geneva Convention, POWs were allowed to receive letters and gifts of food, clothes, and books from home. These parcels were organized by the International Red Cross, which operated from Geneva in neutral Switzerland. Their arrival was eagerly awaited, as they kept prisoners in touch with their families and brought treats to eat.

Food parcels contained luxuries not available in camp

CAMP CROCODILES

These German prisoners were captured by the Allies in Normandy in June 1944. They were brought across the English Channel, then marched in line to a nearby camp. POWs often travelled hundreds of miles to reach a camp. Italians captured in North Africa were taken to Australia, South Africa, and India, while 50,000 more Italians went to the US.

LIVING WITH THE ENEMY

After peace was declared, not all prisoners were returned home immediately. They were, however, allowed to befriend the locals. Sometimes romance blossomed. Ludwig Maier (second right), a German architect imprisoned in Scotland, wed English woman Lucy Tupper in 1947. He had to wait another year before being released.

HAPPY TO BE ALIVE

In April 1945, 9,000 Soviet POWs were freed by the US from the German Stalag 326 camp (below). Sadly, 30,000 captives had already died there. Soviet POWs were treated appallingly by their German captors. They were made to walk for weeks from the Eastern front to German camps. Once there, they were given starvation rations.

Code-breakers

A CODE REPLACES the words of a message with letters, numbers, or symbols. A cipher is a form of code which adds or substitutes letters or numbers in a message to disguise it. Both the Allies and the Axis used codes and ciphers extensively during the war. Messages from the Japanese Purple and the German Enigma cipher machines were successfully deciphered, however, by US and European cryptographers (code-breakers) respectively. Valuable military and diplomatic information then fell into Allied hands, giving them considerable advantage over their enemies.

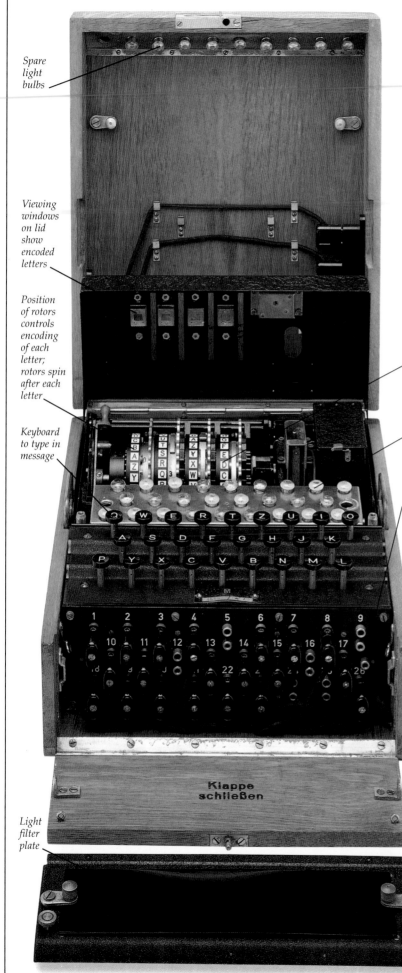

Spare light bulbs

Viewing windows on lid show encoded letters

Position of rotors controls encoding of each letter; rotors spin after each letter

Keyboard to type in message

Light filter plate

Klappe schließen

Rotor cylinder carries three or later four alphabetical rotors

Alphabetical lightboard shows final encoded letter

Plugboard settings are changed daily

ALAN TURING
Mathematician Alan Turing (1912–54) was among the many brilliant people working for British Intelligence during the war. He played a key role in deciphering Enigma, and his work on computer theory and artificial intelligence led to the development of modern computers.

EARLY COMPUTERS
Scientists and cryptographers at the British code-breaking centre, Bletchley Park, developed the "bombe" to decipher the first German Enigma messages. The "bombe" could test every possible combination of rotor positions used by Enigma. As Enigma grew more complex, the British built Colossus, a forerunner of modern electronic computers.

THE ENIGMA CIPHER
The German Enigma machine was first used in 1923 to encode commercial secrets. It was later developed and refined to become the main diplomatic and military cipher machine in use during World War II. Enigma enciphered each letter separately. It did this through a series of alphabetical rotors placed on a cylinder in a predetermined order, and a set of plugs inserted into a plugboard. The settings were varied each day, giving millions of possible combinations.

AN INSIDE RING
Everyday objects, such as this ring, were used during the war to hide microdots. A microdot is a tiny photograph of a coded message, which is so small that it can only be read with a magnifying viewer. Messages must be blown up to actual size for decoding.

Secret chamber

Screw top

Boris Hagelin demonstrates his Converter M-209

FACT TO FICTION
Some of those involved in code-breaking and intelligence during the war later turned their experiences into fiction. One of these was Ian Fleming (1908–64), who worked for British Naval Intelligence.

Ian Fleming, creator of the fictional spy James Bond

THE CONVERTED
During the 1930s, Swedish cryptographer, Boris Hagelin (1892–1983) invented the Converter M-209. It was the main cipher machine used by the US Army during the war. More than 140,000 of these machines were produced for US forces.

Reading aperture

Top cover in open position

Switching unit

Compartment for stepping switches

Stepping switch

PURPLE CIPHER
The Japanese Purple machine used a plugboard and telephone switches to create a device as complex as the German Enigma. US Intelligence cracked Purple's code in September 1940 and built a replica of the mechanism.

Pearl Harbor following the Japanese attack

Spring motor

Concentric discs

Indicating discs

KRYHA CIPHER
The Kryha, invented in 1924, used a spring-driven alphabetic rotor to encode messages. Each letter was substituted by a different one every time the letter was used in a word, making it difficult to decipher. German diplomats used the Kryha during the war, not realizing that the Americans had already broken its code.

IGNORED INFORMATION
Diplomatic communications sent by the Japanese Purple cipher machine were intercepted and decoded by the US. The message warned of a Japanese attack in late 1941, but it was not clear that Pearl Harbor in Hawaii was the target until it was too late. Effective code-breaking during 1942, however, enabled the US to defeat the Japanese navy at the crucial Battle of Midway.

America in the war

Pocket-sized novel for US troops

After the shock of Pearl Harbor, the United States transformed its economy into a giant war machine. As US President Franklin Roosevelt said, the economy became the "arsenal of democracy". The country mass-produced every type of weapon necessary to fight and win on land, sea, and air. Expenditure on war production rose massively, unemployment disappeared, wages doubled, and while there was rationing, it was far less severe than in other countries at war. Unlike every other country at war, the US boomed and most people had more money to spend than ever before.

MASS PRODUCTION
Aircraft factories, such as this Boeing plant in Seattle, played a major role in turning out arms for the war effort. In total, the US factories built more than 250,000 aircraft, 90,000 tanks, 350 destroyer ships, and 200 submarines. By 1944, forty per cent of the world's arms were produced in the US.

BROWNING MACHINE GUN
The 0.5 Browning machine gun was the standard weapon used in US bombers. The Boeing B-17 Flying Fortress, for example, carried 13 such guns. But even flying in close formation with other bombers, the Browning was often no match against attacking German fighter planes.

Spring-loaded pilot parachute

Four main parachutes for a gentle descent

Steel parachute cable

15th Air Force

9th Air Force

US Strategic Air Forces

FIGHTING WITH FIRE
A US marine, his face smeared with protective cream, uses a flame-thrower during bitter fighting on Guadalcanal in the Pacific, 1942. Flame-throwers were often used to set light to buildings or to destroy protective vegetation in order to flush out the enemy.

AIR FORCES
These US Army Air Force (USAAF) sleeve badges represent various divisions. The 15th Air Force was set up to bomb German-held targets from bases in southern Italy. The 9th supported Allied operations in North Africa and Italy. The 8th, 9th, and 15th Air Forces later merged to form the US Strategic Air Forces in Europe.

Crashpan to cushion wheels on landing

The Mustang had a range of 3,347 km (2,080 miles)

Mustangs had a maximum speed of 703 kph (437 mph)

AIR BREAK
Resting between missions, these P-51 Mustang pilots were part of the 15th US Air Force, based in southern Italy.

B-24 LIBERATOR
Having flown all the way from southern Italy, this B-24 Liberator is flying low as it bombs oilfields in Ploesti, southern Romania. The B-24 was a heavy bomber with a long range, able to undertake missions far into German-occupied Europe.

Droppable fuel tank

LONG-RANGE FIGHTER
The P-51 Mustang was one of the best fighter planes of the war. Early versions were limited in their altitude and range. However, after it was re-equipped with a better engine, larger fuel tanks, and a cut-down rear fuselage, the fourth version (P-51 D) became a superb fighter. It was used to escort and defend bombers on their long-range missions over Germany.

North American P-51 D Mustang

Central support to which parachutes are attached

Machine gun

Bag for empty cartridge cases

PARACHUTE JEEP
US Army jeeps, such as this paradroppable version, were dropped by parachute during special operations or major airborne landing. Developed in 1940, the US jeep was one of the best loved of all war vehicles, and the most envied. Its four-wheel drive made it hugely versatile in almost all terrains.

Protective headgear used in turrets and other combat positions where standard helmets were too big

US aircrew M4 helmet

US jeep could carry a 360kg (800 lb) load and tow an anti-tank gun at the same time

Flak jacket weighed 9 kg (20 lb)

Supporting cradle

Parachute release stand

TAKING THE FLAK
This reinforced flak jacket was worn by US aircrew to protect them from anti-aircraft fire. They were introduced in 1942. By 1944, 13,500 were used by the 8th Air Force, which bombed German-held territory in Europe.

Women at work

Before the outbreak of World War II, most women still worked within the home. With men away fighting, however, women became the main workforce. Almost every task that had previously been restricted to men was now taken over by women. Such jobs included bus conductors, train signal operators, drivers, mechanics, clerical workers, shipwrights, and engineers. Women also played an important role in resistance forces and some joined special operations carried out in enemy territory. The war could not have been waged and won without women's vital contribution. After the war, attitudes towards women in the workplace changed forever.

Hilf siegen
als Luftnachrichtenhelferin

NEW RECRUITS
As more men were required for fighting, posters were used to attract increasing numbers of women into the war effort. This one portrays a glamorous image of life as a Luftwaffe (German air force) auxiliary.

A woman assists with aircraft maintenance

LAND GIRLS
One of women's major contributions to the war effort was to take over the running of the farms and grow much-needed food. In Britain the Women's Land Army recruited some 77,000 members to carry out arduous tasks, such as ploughing and harvesting.

AIRCRAFT MAINTENANCE
The shortage of male pilots and mechanics meant that many women learned to fly and maintain planes during the war. They delivered new planes from the factories to the military airfields and played a major role in servicing and preparing planes between missions.

PARACHUTE MAKERS
Seamstresses worked long hours to meet the constant demand for parachutes. Many thousands of parachutes were required by all the armed services. They were used by fighter and bomber pilots if they had to bail out of their aircraft, and by airborne troops dropped into battle from the skies above.

NIGHT WATCH
Many women operated the powerful searchlights that tracked incoming enemy bombers. Once a plane was located, anti-aircraft guns opened fire in an attempt to destroy it before it dropped its deadly bombs. Although some women prepared anti-aircraft guns, they were not allowed to actually fire them. Apart from working for the anti-aircraft command, night work could mean patrolling the streets as an air-raid warden.

Female searchlight operator scours the night sky for enemy bombers

GAS BAG
The threat of gas attacks in Britain meant that everyone had to carry a gas mask with them at all times. This elegant lady's handbag has a special compartment for concealing the owner's mask. Most people, however, carried their masks in cardboard boxes, which women often decorated with fabric.

Gas mask chamber

PANS TO PLANES
Due to the scarcity of iron, tin, and aluminium, wartime posters appealed to housewives to donate unwanted household items. Old pots and pans were melted down to make planes. Iron railings from parks and gardens, old cars, and scrap metal were used to make ships. Even old woollen clothes were unravelled and knitted into socks and scarves for the troops.

Frying pan made from the wreckage of a German plane

FLYING PAN
Crashed enemy planes were sometimes recycled, finishing up as pans and other useful household utensils.

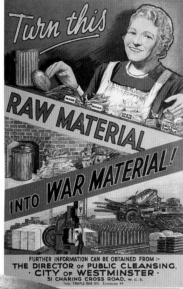

Turn this RAW MATERIAL into WAR MATERIAL!

FURTHER INFORMATION CAN BE OBTAINED FROM :-
THE DIRECTOR of PUBLIC CLEANSING,
· CITY of WESTMINSTER ·
51 CHARING CROSS ROAD, w.c.2.
Tels. TEMPLE BAR 0111   Extension 44

ROSIE THE RIVETER
In the US, fictional character Rosie the Riveter became a national symbol of the new working woman. The women were needed to enter the factories to replace the 16 million US citizens called into the armed services. American women's new jobs included making bombs and aeroplanes, ships and tanks, and running the railways and other vital services.

"Rosie the Riveter", painted by Norman Rockwell for the Saturday Evening Post, May 1943

AIR-RAID TRAINING
In India, fear of a Japanese invasion led the government to take precautionary steps. These women in Bombay are training for air-raid precaution (ARP) duties. Others trained as auxiliaries to support the troops fighting in the Far East.

A wartime childhood

ACROSS THE WORLD, children from every country involved in the war were as affected by the fighting as their parents and grandparents. Their homes were bombed or burned, their fathers were called up to fight, and their mothers went to work in factories or war industries. For some children in mainland Europe and eastern Asia, their countries were occupied or fought over by foreign armies. Other children lived with the threat of invasion. For one group of children in particular, the war brought special fear, as the German authorities sought out Jewish children and sent them to their deaths in concentration camps. For children of all ages, no matter which side they belonged to, the war robbed them of education and a normal, happy life.

GROWING UP IN JAPAN
In school, Japanese children were told about the superiority of their country and their duty to fight for their emperor. As the war progressed, military drills became compulsory, and older children had to work in the student labour force. By 1944, US bombers were attacking Japanese cities on an almost daily basis. As a result, more than 450,000 children were evacuated out of the cities, leaving their parents to an uncertain fate.

A wartime version of "happy families"

BLITZ ENTERTAINMENTS
Many themed toys and games, such as this evacuation card game, were produced during the war years. Card games were a very popular way of passing the time during the long hours spent in air-raid shelters.

Head strap

Protective eye piece

Air filter

"Mickey mouse" gas mask

NOVELTY MASKS
Colourful "Mickey Mouse" gas masks were issued to British toddlers to make them more fun to wear. School children were taught to carry their masks with them at all times and shown how to put them on in a hurry.

All evacuees wore labels indicating their destinations

These children are waiting for transportation to their new homes in the countryside

EVACUEES
Around the world, the war separated many youngsters from their families. During the Blitz, thousands of British children went to live with foster families in the countryside, or even overseas. While some children enjoyed their new lives, many were terribly homesick.

Evacuees were allowed to take a favourite toy

NAZI TOYS
Propaganda infected all aspects of German life. Even toys, such as this Nazi model, taught a version of history which glorified the "Aryan" (blond-haired and blue-eyed) race and put down the Jews. Children were taught that Germans were the master race of the world.

Armed child partisan in Leningrad, Russia, 1943

PAPER PLAY
In wartime, toys were in short supply across Europe as all raw materials were needed for making weapons and machines. As a result, children had to make do with simple toys made of cardboard or paper.

Wild animals made of paper

FOR THE MOTHERLAND
As the German army swept into Russia in 1941, many children found themselves orphaned and homeless. Some youths joined the partisan groups fighting the Germans. Children as young as 10 years old played their part by running messages, fetching supplies, and even taking part in ambushes and acts of sabotage.

IN HIDING
Like all Jewish children, Anne Frank (1929–45) faced the horrifying prospect of being rounded up by Nazis and sent to a concentration camp. For two years, she and her family hid in a secret attic in Holland. Anne kept a diary of daily events and of her hopes for the future. But, in August 1944, the family was betrayed. Anne died of typhus in Belsen concentration camp in March 1945.

Hitler Youth membership card

YOUNG NAZIS
Hitler Youth was formed in 1926 as the male youth division of the Nazi Party (girls joined the League of German Girls). Members wore uniforms, held parades, and attended summer camps. In 1943, those aged 16 and over were called up to fight. Younger recruits helped on farms or delivered post.

FORCED TO FOLLOW HITLER
At first, membership of the Hitler Youth was voluntary. But in 1936 all other German youth groups were disbanded. Joining the Hitler Youth was made compulsory for all children aged 10 to 18.

Battle for the Pacific

AFTER THEIR SURPRISE ATTACK on Pearl Harbor in December 1941, the Japanese swarmed all over southeast Asia and the islands of the Pacific Ocean. By May 1942, they had overrun Burma, Malaya (now Malaysia), the Dutch East Indies (now Indonesia), Singapore, and the Philippines, and were advancing island by island across the Pacific, south towards Australia and east to the US. Their aim was to construct a huge economic empire from which Japan could guarantee supplies of oil and other essential raw materials needed to build up military power. Japan seemed invincible, but two massive naval battles – in the Coral Sea in May 1942, and at Midway (in the central Pacific) in June 1942 – halted their advance. Turning the tide against Japan was, however, to prove a lengthy and costly battle for the US forces and both sides experienced heavy casualties.

JAPANESE PRAYER FLAG
All Japanese servicemen carried prayer flags with them into battle. Friends and relatives wrote prayers and blessings on the white background of the flag of Japan. They never wrote on the sun itself, however, which is considered sacred. Some wore these flags around their heads, others carried them in their pockets.

Douglas Devastator bombers prepare for action

AIRCRAFT CARRIER
Douglas Devastator torpedo bombers prepare to take-off from the deck of USS *Enterprise* during the Battle of Midway. Devastators were old and lumbering planes used by the US aboard aircraft carriers. They proved no match for the speedy Japanese Mitsubishi A6M Zero fighters, which knocked out all but four of the *Enterprise*'s bombers. Overall, however, the Japanese suffered a defeat at Midway.

THE CORAL SEA
A wrecked Japanese plane floats in the Coral Sea (north east of Australia). The Japanese were trying to capture island bases to use for air attacks on Australia, but the US fleet halted their advance southwards in May 1942. Coral Sea was the first naval battle conducted entirely by aircraft taking off from carriers. The fleets never met.

A Japanese aircraft floats in tatters after being shot out of the sky

STRUGGLE FOR GUADALCANAL ISLAND

US aircraft carrier *Hornet* comes under heavy fire from Japanese aircraft during the Battle of Santa Cruz in October 1942. This sea battle was one of many fought around Guadalcanal (one of the Solomon Islands to the east of New Guinea) as Japanese and US forces struggled to gain control of this strategic base. The US eventually forced the Japanese off the island in February 1943, but the ferocity of the Japanese resistance showed how far they were prepared to go to defend newly won territory.

JAPANESE NAVAL SEXTANTS

Sextants were essential to the Japanese Navy for navigating around the vast Pacific Ocean. The third-largest in the world, after Britain and the US, the Japanese navy possessed 10 aircraft carriers, 12 massive battleships, 36 cruisers, more than 100 destroyers, and a powerful naval air force.

Scale showing degrees north or south of equator

SUICIDE MISSIONS

As the battle for the Philippines raged in October 1944, in a measure of desperation the Japanese introduced a terrifying weapon. A special unit of volunteer bomber pilots (Kamikazes) flew planes loaded with explosives onto the decks of US warships to blow them up. Kamikazes were never in short supply – 700 attacked the US fleet off Okinawa on 6 April 1945.

Adjustable eyepiece

Japanese naval sextant for calculating latitude (distance north or south)

Horizon mirror

Kamikaze pilot ties a hachimaki around his head

FLYING MASK

Japanese pilots wore leather masks to protect their faces while flying. The masks made them look even fiercer than their warlike reputation suggested. Few pilots were ever captured by the Allies, as most preferred to kill themselves rather than surrender.

KAMIKAZE PILOT

Japanese pilots volunteered to join Kamikaze flights, knowing that this meant certain death. Kamikaze means "divine wind" and some considered it glorious to die for their emperor. Other pilots were inspired by Japanese military traditions of self-sacrifice. They wore the ritual *hachimaki* (headcloth) of the fierce Samurai warriors of ancient Japan.

Japan at war

Australian
sub-machine gun

Japanese naval and military ensign

THROUGHOUT the war, the Japanese empire was fighting on three fronts. In the north, Chinese armies were fighting to rid their country of its Japanese occupiers. In the south and east, US, Australian and New Zealand forces hopped from island to island across the Pacific Ocean as they fought to drive out Japanese forces and to establish air and naval bases close to Japan. In the southwest, a "forgotten war" continued to be fought in the jungles of Burma. Here, the British army and the Chindits (a British-Burmese fighting unit) under Major General Orde Wingate, fought the Japanese army to liberate Burma. In all these battles, many Japanese soldiers fought to the death, making them a formidable enemy.

DEFENDING AUSTRALIA
Australian forces were heavily involved in the war against Japan. This was because their country was directly threatened by Japanese expansion in southeast Asia. Australia played an important role in preventing the Japanese from occupying Papua New Guinea in 1942 and they fought alongside US forces, liberating New Guinea and other islands.

A Japanese soldier holds the flag, known as the Rising Sun

24-HOUR RATIONS
British forces fighting in the Pacific and southeast Asia were issued with food packs like the one pictured. Although the food was far from exciting, a pack provided one man with enough nourishment for an entire day.

LOYAL FIGHTERS
More than 1,700,000 Japanese soldiers obeyed the Soldier Code of 1942. It was based on the ancient Bushido (warrior) Code of the samurai fighters. This stated that soldiers must be totally loyal to the emperor and it was their duty to die rather than face the shame of capture. As a result, Japanese soldiers were often fanatical fighters dedicated to achieving victory at all costs.

US Army
field
telephone

PORTABLE COMMUNICATIONS
Field telephones were used by Allied and Japanese soldiers to keep in contact with their commanders and the rest of their unit. The speed of the Japanese advance across southeast Asia and the Pacific meant that troops needed efficient communications to inform headquarters of their progress, and on the whereabouts of the enemy.

LIBERATING BURMA
The decisive battle for Burma was fought on the road between the cities of Kohima and Imphal, both just over the border in India. The British had used Imphal as their base to regroup and rearm following their expulsion from Burma by the Japanese in May 1942. The Japanese decided to attack first, and invaded India in March 1944. British and Indian troops (right) fought back and defeated a force of 80,000 Japanese. This opened the way for the liberation of Burma itself, which was eventually achieved in May 1945.

THE THAILAND–BURMA RAILWAY
Diesel-powered traction cars that could run on rails or roads were used by the Japanese from 1942 to 1943. With them, the Japanese built a railway from Thailand to the newly conquered Burma. The Japanese intended to use it to move troops and supplies quickly throughout their vast southeast Asian empire.

SAVED FROM STARVATION
These Dutchmen released from a Japanese prisoner-of-war camp in Indonesia in 1945 were some of the lucky ones. About a quarter of the 103,000 Australian, US, British, and Dutch soldiers taken captive by the Japanese had died in camps by 1944. Of these, 12,000 had worked on the Thailand-Burma Railway. Asian prisoners suffered far worse – at least 100,000 died building the railway alone.

BRIDGE ATTACK
The 415-km (258-mile) long Thailand-Burma Railway ran through jungles, mountains and alongside the Kwai Noi River. Railway bridges – such as the one above – were designed and built by prisoners of war. British planes, operating from India, regularly bombed the bridges hoping to destroy the railway and halt the Japanese.

Improvised
spectacles
and comb

A US memorial shows marines hoisting the flag on Mt Suribachi, Iwo Jima

CAPTURED BY THE JAPANESE
Prisoners of war (POWS) held by the Japanese had to make their own everyday essentials as they were given few provisions by their captors. The Japanese had no respect for POWs, and worked many of them to death building railways, roads, and bridges.

RAISING THE FLAG ON IWO JIMA
In February 1945 US marines stormed Iwo Jima, a tiny island south of Japan. The Japanese defended the island to the bitter end. Of 21,000 soldiers, only 216 were taken prisoner. The rest died fighting. After suffering heavy losses at Iwo Jima and on Okinawa, the US started bombing mainland Japanese cities, and later dropped two atomic bombs, on Hiroshima and Nagasaki.

The Battle of the Atlantic

THROUGHOUT THE WAR, a fierce battle raged between the Allies and the Germans in the icy waters of the North Atlantic Ocean. As Allied sailors braved the elements to bring vital supplies from the US into British ports, German U-boats (submarines) and destroyers attacked at every opportunity. The German navy was small compared to that of the Allies, but its submarine fleet was capable of inflicting great damage. At first the U-boats reigned supreme. They sank 2 million tonnes of Allied shipping in the first four months of 1941 alone and more than 5.4 million tonnes in 1942. However, the Allies' greater use of the convoy system, long-range aircraft patrols, quick-response anti-submarine warships, and improved radar made the U-boats increasingly vulnerable. By mid-1943, with 95 U-boats lost in just three months, the tide of the battle turned in the Allies' favour and the Atlantic became safer for shipping once more.

DIG FOR VICTORY
Overseas imports of food were severely hampered by the war. In Britain, to ensure sufficient supplies of fruit and vegetables, a "Dig for Victory" campaign was launched urging people to grow as much food as possible. Every spare bit of fertile land, including gardens and parks, was cultivated into vegetable patches.

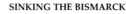

Equipped with 88 guns including 20 long-range and 68 anti-aircraft guns

Periscope

Wet-and-dry exit and re-entry chamber

SINKING THE BISMARCK
One of the largest battleships in the German navy was the *Bismarck*, which the Germans claimed to be unsinkable. The ship set off from Gdynia in the Baltic on 18 May 1941. It sailed in a huge loop around the top of Iceland, where it sank the British *HMS Hood*, before it was caught and destroyed by a British fleet on 27 May. All but 115 of the *Bismarck*'s crew of 2,222 lost their lives.

Main steering wheel

Helmsman's seat

First lieutenant's seat frame

INSIDE A MIDGET
The British X-craft midget submarine, crewed by a team of four, handled many special missions during the Battle of the Atlantic. Using explosive charges, one attacked and successfully disabled the German battleship *Tirpitz* off the coast of Norway in September 1943. The *Tirpitz* had presented a great potential threat to convoys heading north from Britain to Russia.

Periscope

THE BIBER
Armed with two torpedoes, German Biber submarines operated off the coast of northern France and the Netherlands between 1944 and 1945. Bibers caused damage to Allied cargo and cross-Channel ships supplying invasion forces in western Europe.

Viewing port

Distilled water tank

Wooden deckboard

Log tank

Cradle for oxygen bottle

Freshwater tank

Towing eye

Warhead

> *"We all snapped our hands to our caps, glanced at the flag, and jumped ... In the water we were pushed together in a bunch, as we bobbed up and down like corks."*
>
> LIEUTENANT BURKHARD VON MULLENHEIM-RECHBERG, *BISMARCK* SURVIVOR

UP PERISCOPE

While lurking just beneath the surface, U-boat crew members used periscopes to watch the progress of Allied convoys. From this position of relative safety they could select targets for their guns and deadly torpedoes. When U-boats were close to or on the surface, however, they were easily detectable from the air, and many were destroyed by Allied planes.

U-boat officer uses a periscope to locate enemy ships

The ship was 251 m (823 ft) long

Gun is aimed ready to fire at enemy ships and U-boats

UNDER ATTACK

Only 30 crew members of this floundering German U-boat survived an attack from a US navy ship. When underwater, U-boats were vulnerable to attack from depth charges dropped from Allied ships or aircraft. On the surface, they risked attack from bombs, torpedoes, or shells, and in shallow waters, mines were also a hazard. Out of 39,000 German submariners, only 11,000 survived the war.

Torpedo

A sailor on board a warship accompanying an Atlantic convoy keeps a lookout for enemy aircraft

Rudder

Propeller

ATLANTIC CONVOY

Single merchant ships crossing the North Atlantic were highly vulnerable to attack from waiting U-boats. As a result, they travelled in large convoys protected by escorting warships and, where possible, air cover. Convoys travelled at the speed of their slowest member, however, making the North Atlantic crossing a dangerous exercise in which many sailors lost their lives.

Road to Stalingrad

German bronze
tank assault badge

GERMANY INVADED the Soviet Union in 1941. It advanced in three directions – north towards Leningrad, east towards Moscow, and south to the wheat fields and oil wells of Ukraine and the Caucasus. To achieve success in the south, the Germans had to capture Stalingrad on the Volga River. For Hitler, this city was of huge importance as it was named after the Soviet leader, Stalin. For similar reasons Stalin was equally determined that the city should not be lost. The battle for Stalingrad was intense, with vast losses on both sides. The eventual destruction of the attacking German army and its surrender, in early 1943, marked a turning point in the war. No longer was the German army unbeatable.

IN THE SNOW
War in the Soviet Union was aggravated for both sides by the Russian winter. As temperatures dropped below freezing, the Germans were ill-equipped for the extreme cold. The Russians, however, were more used to the temperature and better equipped with white camouflaged oversuits, quilted undersuits, fur hats, and felt boots.

RED ARMY WEAPONRY
Many thousands of sub-machine guns, such as this PPSh-1941, were issued to the Red Army during the war. They were produced cheaply and quickly for use while fighting at close quarters.

Trigger

Hooded foresight

Forward hand grip

Hand grip

Soviet sub-machine gun

Shoulder butt

HAND GRENADES
Soviets used hand grenades to stop the enemy advancing into Stalingrad. Wounded soldiers sometimes had to pull pins out with their teeth before hurling the grenades.

STANDARD ISSUE
The 7.62 mm (0.3 in) Tokarev TT33 semi-automatic pistol was the standard issue gun given to Soviet officers, airmen, and tank crews. If a tank was disabled, the crew would have some means of defence.

BATTLE OF STALINGRAD
The battle for Stalingrad began in August 1942. The German 6th Army attacked the city from the west and pushed the defenders into a thin line of houses and factories along the Volga River. The Soviets counterattacked on 19 November and soon encircled the 6th Army. The Germans tried to rescue their besieged army, but were forced to surrender on 2 February 1943.

SHOOT-OUT
Germans and Soviets fought over every building in Stalingrad. The two sides sometimes even occupied different floors of the same building. Hand-to-hand fighting was widespread, and anyone showing their head above ground was likely to be killed by sniper fire.

RED ARMY CAVALRY
The Red Army infantry was supported by cavalry divisions that were able to move quickly to the front line. Both sides used horses to tow artillery and wagons laden with supplies. Horses were a hindrance in winter, however, as they were easily bogged down by wet mud or snow.

Red Army cavalry brandish swords as they charge through the snow

T-34 was armed with an 85 mm gun after 1943

German soldiers suffer a harsh Soviet winter

THE CASUALTIES
About 91,000 German soldiers were rounded up and imprisoned at the end of the battle of Stalingrad. The fighting led to an appalling number of casualties. Both sides lost about 500,000 soldiers each. An estimated 2 million Stalingrad civilians lost their lives. Amazingly, 10,000 civilians lived in the city throughout the battle and survived.

TANK SUPERIOR
The Soviet T-34 tank, designed in 1939, was the mainstay of the Red Army armoured units. A total of 39,698 were built between 1941 and 1945. These tanks carried a crew of five – one commander, two gunners, one loader, and a driver. Conditions inside, however, were cramped. With a maximum speed of 51 kph (32 mph) the tank could cover up to 400 km (250 miles) without refuelling. German tanks, with their slower speeds and smaller range were no match for the all-conquering T-34.

Gun mounted in swivelling turret

T-34 diesel engine functions well in severe cold

Straw boots worn by German sentries in the Soviet Union

Total weight 32,514 kg (32 tons)

FROSTBITE
German soldiers fighting in the Soviet Union fashioned snow boots out of straw in a vain attempt to keep their feet warm and dry. Many suffered from frostbite during the harsh Russian winters. Ordinary clothes were inadequate and their stiff leather boots were too tight to allow them to wear layers of socks and too porous to keep out the damp.

Wide tracks are ideal for crossing soft, uneven terrain

Inside the Soviet Union

THE WAR HAD AN IMMENSE impact on the Soviet Union. Although it had spent almost two years getting ready for war, nothing could have prepared the nation for the amount of suffering inflicted upon it. In order to keep industries safe from attack, 1,500 factories were moved in their entirety hundreds of kilometres east across the Ural mountains. Six million workers followed them. Millions more were enslaved by the Germans, or killed in work camps. A total of 20 million Soviets died. Yet the civilian population rallied to save their country, and worked hard for victory. The war became known as the Great Patriotic War.

RESISTANCE FIGHTERS
Posters urged Soviets living in German-occupied territory to join the partisans and *"Beat the enemy mercilessly"*. Groups of partisans who lived in the forests ambushed German convoys and attacked command posts and lines of communication.

Red Star   Red Banner

RED ARMY AWARDS
The major medals awarded to Soviet soldiers were the Hero of the Soviet Union and the Orders of the Red Banner and the Red Star. Stalin introduced the Orders of Kutuzov and Suvorov, named after 19th-century field marshals who fought off invasions by the Poles, Turks, and Napoleonic France.

Residents of Leningrad abandon their homes destroyed by Nazi bombs

WATER, WATER EVERYWHERE ...
During the Soviet winter of 1941, the temperature in Leningrad fell to -40°C (-40°F). Food ran out and water supplies froze. People had to gather snow and ice to thaw. One local recalled: "We couldn't wash ourselves because we were only strong enough to fetch water to drink."

THE SIEGE OF LENINGRAD
The longest siege of the war took place in the Soviet city of Leningrad. German troops, supported by Finns, surrounded the city in September 1941. Finland had joined the war on Germany's side to gain revenge for its defeat by the Soviets the previous year. The Germans dropped more than 100,000 bombs and 200,000 shells on Leningrad. Despite killing 200,000 citizens, they failed to capture the city. The siege was eventually lifted by the Red Army in January 1944, 890 days after it began.

Harvesting vegetables in a cathedral square, Leningrad

FEEDING THE CITY

During the Leningrad siege, the biggest threats to inhabitants were cold and hunger. Every spare bit of ground was used to grow food, such as cabbages and potatoes, but rationing remained strict throughout the siege. In total, more than 630,000 civilians died from starvation and the extreme cold.

Mayakovsky Metro station in Moscow being used as an air-raid shelter

This poster of 1942 urged Soviets to *"Follow this worker's example, produce more for the front"*

ATTACK ON MOSCOW

In October 1941, as German troops attacked the Soviet city of Moscow, many civilians sheltered in the Metro station. Others tried to flee. But the Germans were running out of supplies and were unable to cope with the severe Soviet winter. In December 1941, the Russians counterattacked and the Germans pulled back their forces. The Soviet capital was saved.

SNIPERS

Among the many wartime heroes were the Red Army snipers engaged to shoot the enemy one by one. The exploits of the Stalingrad snipers became legendary. When a sniper achieved 40 kills, he was given the title of "noble sniper".

Soviet sniper rifle

Wooden hand-guard

Foresight

PRODUCE MORE!

Despite the the strong male image on this poster, more than half of the Soviet workforce by the end of the war was female. Soviet civilians played a huge role in the defeat of Hitler. They worked hard in the factories to increase the production of armaments and essential war equipment.

THE MOLOTOV COCKTAIL

During the Russo-Finnish War, Finnish troops hurled home-made petrol bombs at Russian tanks. They called the bombs Molotov cocktails after Soviet politician Vyacheslav Molotov (1890–1986), whom they held largely responsible for the war.

THE RUSSO-FINNISH WAR

After Germany invaded Poland in 1939, the Soviet Union tried to secure its western frontier. In November 1939, the Soviet army invaded Finland, its western neighbour. The Finns fought back with great courage. But in March 1940, they were forced to accept a peace treaty and loss of land. The Soviets lost more than 80,000 soldiers against Finnish losses of only 25,000. This revealed the weakness of the Red Army.

Finnish Lahti 20 mm L39 anti-tank rifle

Wooden cheek-rest

Rubber recoil pad

Fighting in the desert

In JUNE 1940, Mussolini's Italy entered the war on the German side and in September invaded Egypt from its colony of Libya. Within months, the British army had overwhelmed the Italians, taking 130,000 soldiers prisoner. Alarmed at the collapse of their Italian allies, Germany began to send troops to North Africa in February 1941. For almost two years, the battle was fought across the desert until the British Eighth Army achieved a massive victory over the German Afrika Korps at El Alamein in November 1942. The same month, US and British troops landed in Algeria and Morocco. They advanced eastwards to surround the westward-retreating Germans. By May 1943, the Afrika Korps and their Italian allies were forced to surrender. The Allies could now turn their attention back to Europe.

SLY DESERT FOX
Field Marshal Erwin Rommel (1891–1944), far left, commander of the German Afrika Korps, was known as the Desert Fox. He had the ability to quickly assess a situation and "sniff" out his enemy's weak points. Germans and British respected him, the latter because he was known to treat his prisoners well. In 1944 Rommel took his own life after he was implicated in a plot to murder Hitler.

BATTLE OF TOBRUK
The Mediterranean port of Tobruk, in eastern Libya, was the scene of some of the fiercest fighting of the desert war. The city was first held by the Italians, then captured by the British in early 1941. Later that year it was besieged by the Germans, who seized control in June 1942. The British recaptured it after El Alamein in November 1942.

British troops advancing in the sand at El Alamein

BATTLE OF EL ALAMEIN
By October 1942, the German Afrika Korps had reached El Alamein. It was an important coastal town, the gateway to Egypt and the Suez Canal (a vital international shipping lane linking the Mediterranean to the Red Sea). Here the Afrika Korps met the British Eighth Army, which eventually defeated them in an exhausting 12-day infantry, tank, and artillery battle. The victory – the first major British land success against Germany – marked a turning point in the war.

German anti-tank mine

British mine detector

MINE ALERT
Vast minefields were laid around El Alamein by both sides. The mines caused many deaths as tanks and infantry columns tried to negotiate their way around them. Although many were detonated during and after the war, a vast number of unexploded mines still remain buried in the desert.

ON THE LOOKOUT IN LIBYA
The German Afrika Korps was formed in 1941 to assist Italians in North Africa. Here, one of its members uses "donkey's ears binoculars" to view the enemy. Although superbly led by Rommel, the Afrika Korps relied on Mediterranean convoys for reinforcements and supplies, and these were attacked by the British.

INVASION OF SICILY
Allied troops bring vehicles and supplies ashore after their invasion of Sicily in July 1943. The German defeat in North Africa had opened the way for the Allies to invade Europe, but the Allies did not think they were powerful enough to risk a direct attack against German forces. Instead, they decided to invade Italy in the hope of forcing it out of the war.

HELP FROM THE COMMONWEALTH
Some New Zealand troopers and other special units fighting in North Africa wore Arab-style cloth headwear to suit the hot conditions. New Zealand units joined the British Eighth Army, including a Maori (native New Zealander) battalion, which made its mark in North Africa and Italy.

Cloth wrap kept out sand and sun

RATS TO THE RESCUE
The British Eighth Army in North Africa was lead by Field Marshal Montgomery (1887–1976), above. Monty's attention to detail and concern for troop morale led his army to victory at El Alamein. Soldiers in part of the army, the 7th Armoured Division, were nicknamed the Desert Rats.

Inside, a crew of six manned the tank

Camouflaged in desert colours

MONTY'S TANK
Montgomery (see above) had his own tank, a US Grant M3A3. He used it for forward observation on the battlefields of North Africa, and then in the invasion of Sicily and Italy. Similar tanks played a major role in defeating Rommel's army.

Propaganda and morale

THE WAR WAS FOUGHT with propaganda (spreading ideas) as much as ammunition, for both Allied and Axis nations needed to convince their own people that the war was right and that their side would win. The line between truth and propaganda was very fine. Both sides manipulated public opinion in order to keep up the morale of the civilian population at home and the forces fighting abroad. It was also used in an attempt to break down the morale of the enemy. Some propaganda was crude, some was subtle, but as Josef Göbbels, the German propaganda minister, stated: "A good government cannot survive without good propaganda." Films, radio (there was little television during the war), leaflets, and posters were all used in the battle for hearts and minds, while entertainers travelled the world singing to homesick troops.

HITLER THE LEADER
Propaganda played a huge role in Hitler's success. It did much to boost his image as a visionary leader of his people. He was often shown surrounded by adoring followers, depicted as a great statesman who would take his people to world domination.

TOKYO ROSE
In 1943–44 Mrs Iva Ikuko Toguri D'Aquino, an American with Japanese parents, broadcast daily 15-minute radio shows from Tokyo. They were full of nostalgia designed to demoralize US troops in the Pacific, making them feel so homesick they would lose the will to fight. She called them "fighting orphans". The troops actually enjoyed her programmes which became a target for sarcastic humour, and gave her the nickname Tokyo Rose. After the war, she was sentenced to 10 years in prison for treason.

British airmen load up with propaganda fliers

BOMBARDING THE ENEMY WITH IDEAS
These anti-Nazi leaflets are being taken on to British RAF planes to drop over Vienna and Prague. During the war, British and US bombers dropped nearly 6 billion leaflets over occupied Europe. Some were aimed at the civilians of an occupied country warning them against co-operating with the enemy. Others told soldiers that their efforts were futile and urged them to disobey their orders or to surrender.

An umbrella is used to caricature the British soldier

Japanese uniform and insignia

German armband

KICK OUT THE BRITS
The British are the butt of this Italian cartoon from 1942. Italians wanted the Mediterranean to be an "Italian lake" and were attempting to kick the British out of North Africa. It shows the Germans doing the same in Europe and the Japanese ousting the British from Asia. The three Axis powers are seen to have a common cause.

AFRICA

MEDITERRANEO

EUROPA

ASIA

French Tricolour

ALLIED POWER
The simplest visual images were often the most effective propaganda tools. This US poster of 1943 is a perfect example – it shows the four Allied nations pulling apart the Nazi swastika. Constant reminders that the combined strength of the allied nations would overcome the Axis did much to lift morale in even the darkest days of the war.

British Union Jack

USSR Hammer and sickle on Red Flag

US Stars and Stripes

Vera Lynn signs autographs for Dutch sailors

SAMURAI DESTROYER
This poster celebrates the Axis' might after Japan had sunk two British warships. Japan, portrayed as an ancient Samurai warrior, destroyed HMS *Prince of Wales* and HMS *Repulse* which were defending Singapore from invasion in December 1941.

US WAR GODS
A Chinese leaflet issued in early 1945 reads: "This American pilot helped you to chase the Japanese out of the Chinese sky ... but he and his Chinese colleagues need your help when they are hurt or lost or hungry." Such appeals were necessary to tell rural Chinese people which nations were friendly.

ENTERTAINING THE TROOPS
British singer Vera Lynn, the "forces' sweetheart", was one of many entertainers who performed to the troops to keep their morale high. The popular songs of the day were quiet and sentimental, soothing shattered nerves and reassuring soldiers that they would soon be returning home.

The Holocaust

OF THE MANY HORRORS committed during the war, the Holocaust – the Nazi attempt to exterminate Europe's Jews – is the most shocking of all. The Nazis were deeply anti-Semitic (prejudiced against Jews). They sent thousands of Jews to concentration camps, where many were worked to death. Others were forced to live in ghettos. When Russia was invaded in 1941, many millions of non-German Jews fell under Nazi control. The Nazis devised the "Final Solution" to what they saw as the Jewish problem. They set up extermination camps to kill huge numbers of Jews each day. No one knows how many died in this way, but it is likely that more than 6 million Jews were murdered.

ANTI-JEWISH IDEAS
This poster advertises an exhibition called "The Eternal Jew", in Munich, Germany, in 1937. It was one of many methods the Nazis used to spread anti-Semitic ideas. When they took power in 1933, the Nazis boycotted Jewish businesses. In 1935, they passed the Nuremberg Laws, which deprived Jews of their citizenship.

FIRST IMPRESSIONS
Many of the Jews sent by rail to the camps thought they were off to work in Eastern Europe. Some of the victims were told the gas chambers were shower blocks.

WARSAW GHETTO
In 1940, the 445,000 Jews in the Polish capital, Warsaw, were herded into a walled ghetto. The ghetto was then sealed shut. Conditions inside were awful, and many died from illness or starvation. In April 1943, the Nazis attacked the ghetto with tanks and aircraft in order to wipe it out. The Jews fought back to the bitter end, but only about 100 escaped.

Jews are rounded up in the Warsaw ghetto at gunpoint

THE YELLOW STAR
From 1942 onward, Jews in German-occupied Europe had to sew a yellow star onto their clothes. This made it easier for the authorities to identify them. They were also worn in the camps.

EXTERMINATION CAMPS
The Nazis set up concentration camps to hold Jews, communists, political prisoners, gypsies, homosexuals, and others they considered "undesirable". Many prisoners were forced to work in nearby factories. In 1942, eight extermination camps, notably Auschwitz (below) and Treblinka, in Poland, were fitted with gas chambers to speed up the killing of Jews.

Auschwitz concentration camp in Poland is preserved as a permanent reminder of the Holocaust

CREMATORIA
The bodies of dead inmates were stripped of all clothes, hair, jewellery, and any gold teeth, and piled up ready for cremation. The crematoria were run by fellow prisoners. In Auschwitz, some prisoners rebelled against this horrific work by blowing up one of the crematoria.

A Hungarian Jew, one of the survivors of Belsen

Stretchers were used to place bodies in the furnaces

FEEDING BOWL
This empty tin was used as a feeding bowl by a camp inmate. It once contained the cyanide gas crystals used extensively in the gas chambers to kill thousands.

CAMP CONDITIONS
Conditions in the camps were appalling. Food was scarce, and those able to work were forced to endure 12-hour shifts. Many of the officers who ran the camps enjoyed abusing inmates. Others, notably Dr Josef Mengele at Auschwitz, conducted horrific experiments on both living and dead prisoners.

FACING THE TRUTH
Allied troops marched local Germans into some of the camps to confront the atrocities committed in the name of Nazism. As the camps were liberated by the invading Russian, US, and British armies, the true horror of the Holocaust became clear.

SS guards captured at Belsen

PUNISHING THE GUARDS
For the Allied troops liberating the camps, the gruesome reality was too much to bear. When US soldiers entered Dachau in April 1945, they shot 122 German SS guards on sight. Some guards were put to work burying the dead. Some officers were arrested and put on trial for crimes against humanity.

D-Day invasion

"Sword", the codename for one of the D-Day landing beaches

"SWORD" BEACH
This detailed intelligence map of "Sword" beach indicates the physical features and dangers the soldiers would encounter as they waded ashore. "Sword" was the easternmost beach and, like neighbouring "Juno" and "Gold" beaches, was stormed by British and Canadian forces. US forces landed on the western "Omaha" and "Utah" beaches.

IN THE EARLY MORNING of 6 June 1944 (D-Day) the greatest seaborne invasion in history took place on the beaches of Normandy, France. Operation Overlord, as the Allied invasion of France was called, was the result of years of detailed planning. More than 150,000 US, British, and Canadian soldiers were ferried across the English Channel to establish five beachheads (shorelines captured from the enemy). The invasion was almost called off due to bad weather, but eventually the Allied Commander-in-Chief, General Dwight D. Eisenhower (1890–1969), took the risky decision to go ahead. The Germans were expecting an invasion further to the east, and had set up a defence there. By nightfall, the beachheads were secure, and the loss of life – 2,500 soldiers – was minimal for an operation of this scale. The liberation of German-occupied Western Europe had begun.

"OMAHA" INVASION
The most difficult of the five landing sites was "Omaha" beach. It was surrounded by high cliffs and had few routes inland, making it ideal to defend but difficult to attack. The US troops sustained at least 3,000 casualties but managed to establish a 3 km (2 mile) deep beachhead by nightfall.

SKY ATTACK
Parachutists played an important role in the Normandy landings. In the early hours of D-Day, US Army paratroopers dropped behind "Utah" beach to secure vital positions. Meanwhile, British paratroopers landed behind "Sword" beach where they destroyed a German battery (gun site).

MULBERRY HARBOURS
"If we cannot capture a port we must take one with us," remarked a British naval officer. As a result, two floating harbours, or Mulberries, were built in Britain. These were huge floating roadways made from steel sections that were towed across the Channel and slotted together off the "Gold" and "Omaha" beaches.

COLLAPSIBLE MOTORBIKE
Folding motorcycles were dropped behind enemy lines to provide transport for the landing airborne forces. The bikes had a range of 144 km (90 miles) and could travel at up to 48 kph (30 mph).

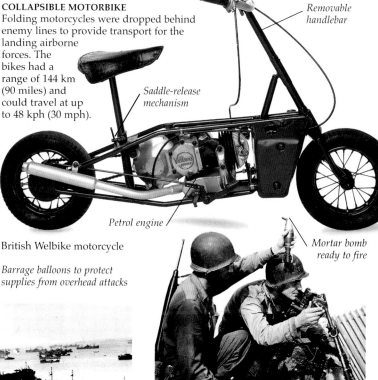

Removable handlebar

Saddle-release mechanism

Petrol engine

British Welbike motorcycle

Barrage balloons to protect supplies from overhead attacks

ON THE BEACH
This view of "Omaha" on the day after D-Day was typical of all five invasion beaches as trucks, tanks, and troops flooded in. Once the first wave of soldiers was ashore, they set about making the beach as safe as possible from enemy attack. Then ships began to unload vast amounts of equipment.

Mortar bomb ready to fire

EXPLOSIVE WORK
Once ashore, the Allies began to press inland, encountering snipers, tanks, and fortifications hidden among the hedgerows of Normandy. Progress was slow, but by the end of July the Allies had nearly one million men in France. They then swept east towards Paris.

Liberation

THE LIBERATION OF EUROPE from German and Italian rule was a long, drawn-out affair. From the first Russian counterattack at Stalingrad in November 1942, the Red Army had slowly pushed the German army eastwards out of Russia. The Polish frontier was not crossed until January 1944, however, and fighting in the Balkans continued into 1945. The Allied liberation of Italy from fascist rule was similarly slow, while the liberation of France did not begin until June 1944. Denmark, Norway, and parts of the Netherlands and Austria remained under Nazi rule until the final German surrender in May 1945. In Asia, only the Philippines, most of Burma, and some islands had been recaptured from the Japanese by the end of the war. Everywhere, local people had to begin their lives again, counting the cost of war amid the ruins of their homes.

Soldiers crawl over the rubble of the monastery at Monte Cassino

LIBERATION OF PARIS

The Free French leader, General de Gaulle, led a victory march down the Champs Elysées in Paris on 26 August 1944. Paris had been occupied by the Germans since 14 June 1940. But, on 19 August 1944, the Resistance rose up and Free French forces stormed the city six days later. German commander, General Choltitz, surrendered.

FALL OF MONTE CASSINO

German paratroopers battle against Allied soldiers in the rubble of the Monte Cassino monastery in Italy, 1944. After the Allied invasion and liberation of Sicily in July 1943, Italy surrendered. In October, Italy changed sides and declared war on Germany, its old ally. German troops then poured into Italy, forcing the Allies to fight their way up the entire length of the country.

Sandbags to absorb bullets

FREED FROM FASCISM

In January 1945, Allied forces advanced into northern Italy where they were helped by partisans of the Resistance Army. These partisans fought to bring down Mussolini's puppet government and expel the Germans from Italy. They liberated Milan and Turin, and were also responsible for the execution of Mussolini in April 1945.

Italian partisans in action during the liberation of Milan

Bronze eagle

Shrapnel ripped a hole through the wing

HITLER'S EAGLE
This massive bronze eagle used to hang in Hitler's official residence in Berlin, the Reichschancellery. Captured by the Russians, a Red Army officer gave it to a British soldier in Berlin in 1946. Its wings still bear the scars of the final battle for Berlin.

FRENCH FREEDOM
As France was liberated, Nazi swastikas were ripped down and replaced with the French tricolour. The liberation of France had begun on D-Day (6 June 1944) and ended as Allied troops pushed eastwards into Germany in early 1945. The Free French led by General de Gaulle established a provisional government to take over from the Germans.

Two women tear down a sign in front of Nazi headquarters in Troyes, France

DENAZIFICATION
As the Germans were thrown out of occupied countries by the Allies, local people set about removing all evidence of their former Nazi rulers. German-language signs were torn down and Nazi symbols erased from buildings as people began to rebuild their shattered countries.

A soldier drags a Nazi flag behind him after the liberation of France

The German national emblem (*Hoheitsabzeichen*)

Swastika surrounded by oak-leaf wreath

Russian soldier raises the Red Flag over the German capital, Berlin

FALL OF BERLIN
On 2 May 1945, two days after Hitler committed suicide, Soviet soldiers clambered onto the roof of the captured Reichstag (German parliament) to raise the Red Flag in victory. It had taken two-and-half years of relentless fighting to push the Germans back from the gates of Stalingrad to the outskirts of Berlin, the German capital.

The atomic bomb

TWO GERMAN scientists discovered the physics behind the atomic bomb as early as 1938. They split a uranium atom and caused a chain reaction of huge potential power. After the US entered the war in 1941, an international team of scientists – many having fled from Nazi Germany – worked to turn this discovery into a bomb. The Manhattan Project, as it was known, was based in Los Alamos, New Mexico, and led by nuclear physicist Robert Oppenheimer (1904–67). By July 1945, the team had developed three bombs. The first was tested successfully over the New Mexico desert on 16 July 1945.

Bottle fused by blast at Hiroshima

ENOLA GAY
US Superfortress bomber, "Enola Gay", set off in the early hours of 6 August 1945. The plane dropped its load over Hiroshima, Japan, at 8.15 am before returning to base.

Powerful twin-propeller engines enabled B-29 to carry heavy bomb loads over long distances

SMALL BUT DEADLY
"Little Boy", a uranium 235-based bomb weighing 4,082 kg (9,000 lb), was the name given to the bomb dropped on Hiroshima. Its explosive power was 2,000 times greater than the blast of any previous bomb.

Little Boy was 3 m (10 ft) long with a diameter of 71 cm (28 in)

Mushroom cloud visible 580 km (360 miles) away

Only a handful of brick buildings survived the blast at Nagasaki

Wind blasts outward at 800 kph (500 mph)

Survivors clutch emergency supplies of rice

HORROR OVER HIROSHIMA
The bomb dropped on Hiroshima exploded 600 m (2,000 ft) above the city. It created a blinding heat flash followed by a blast that radiated out 3.66 km (2.27 miles) and flattened 13 sq km (5 sq miles) of buildings. Within five days, more than 138,661 people died.

BOMBING OF NAGASAKI

On the morning of 9 August 1945, the final atomic bomb was dropped on the southern city of Nagasaki, Japan. The plutonium-based "Fat Man" weighed 4,536 kg (10,000 lb). It was originally intended for Kokura, site of a major military base, but poor weather conditions meant that Nagasaki was substituted at the last moment. About 73,884 people were killed, and 51,000 buildings in the city were either damaged or totally destroyed.

Museum of Science and Industry has remained untouched since August 1945

TWICE TOO OFTEN

Although Hiroshima and Nagasaki were rebuilt after the war, a gutted central area of Hiroshima was left untouched as a memorial to the horrors of atomic weapons. An international anti-nuclear conference has met annually in Hiroshima since 1955.

Cloud rises to 10,000 m (33,000 ft)

> "A shattering flash filled the sky... and the world collapsed around me."
>
> *A HIROSHIMA SURVIVOR*

SURVIVORS

More than 200,000 citizens of Hiroshima and Nagasaki were killed by the bombs. Many more, however, suffered appalling burns and other injuries, including radiation sickness. The long-term effects of radiation, including cancer and leukaemia, on both survivors and their future children, makes it impossible to calculate the exact number of deaths. But it is likely that in Hiroshima alone about 150,000 people died of radiation sickness within five years of the blast.

Japanese prisoners of war learn of their country's surrender

Temperature at ground level reaches 5,000°C (9,000°F)

JAPAN SURRENDERS

On 9 August 1945 – the same day as the Nagasaki bombing – Russia attacked the Japanese by invading Manchuria. That evening the Japanese Supreme War Council met with Emperor Hirohito, but failed to decide on a plan of action. Hirohito then took charge and, on 14 August, accepted the Allied demand for Japan's surrender, provided he could remain as emperor. The next day Hirohito broadcast to the Japanese nation – the first time they had ever heard his voice – telling them of the surrender.

Front page news in Britain

Victory

THE UNCONDITIONAL surrender of German forces took place at 2.41am on 7 May 1945 in a small schoolhouse in Rheims, northern France. It was witnessed by emissaries from the four Allies – Britain, France, the US, and USSR. The ceremony was repeated in Berlin the following day – 8 May – marked officially as VE (Victory in Europe) Day. Three months later, following the dropping of the two atomic bombs on Hiroshima and Nagasaki, Japan surrendered on 14 August. The formal surrender took place on board USS *Missouri* in Tokyo Bay on 2 September 1945. After six years of war, the world was at last at peace. The Allies had drawn up detailed plans to deal with their former enemies, but for a few days, it was time to celebrate.

"East and west have met. This is the news for which the whole Allied world has been waiting. The forces of liberation have joined hands."

US RADIO COMMENTATOR, 1945

FIREWORKS OVER MOSCOW
Moscow celebrated the victory over Nazi Germany with a massive fireworks display and a military parade through Red Square. Captured war trophies, such as Nazi banners, were laid at the feet of the victorious Russian leaders.

JAPAN SURRENDERS
VJ (Victory in Japan) Day, on 15 August 1945, was cause for more celebration throughout the world. But although Japan had officially surrendered, many Japanese troops continued to fight on. It was not until September that peace was finally established.

Indian newspaper printed in English

St George killing the dragon

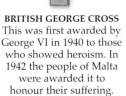

BRITISH GEORGE CROSS
This was first awarded by George VI in 1940 to those who showed heroism. In 1942 the people of Malta were awarded it to honour their suffering.

CROSS OF VALOUR
Polish servicemen who displayed great courage in battle were awarded the Cross of Valour. A Polish eagle sits in the middle of the cross.

VE DAY IN NEW YORK
The day after the unconditional surrender of the German forces on 7 May, the world at last had something to celebrate. Across the USA, people poured onto the streets and held impromptu parties. In London, Prime Minister Winston Churchill appeared on the balcony of Buckingham Palace with the royal family to thousands of cheering people. More joyful celebrations and street parties were held in Paris and other newly liberated cities in Europe.

Ticker-tape streamers add to the party atmosphere in Wall Street, New York

The aftermath

THE COUNTRIES OF THE WORLD faced a huge task in 1945. Both the victors and the vanquished had suffered terrible losses, with an estimated 55 million people losing their lives in battle or on the home front. Worst affected was the USSR, with more than 20 million deaths, and Poland which lost one-fifth of its entire pre-war population. Six million Jews lost their lives in the Holocaust. All countries, with the sole exception of the USA, emerged from the war with their cities bombed or ruined and their factories and farms destroyed. German and Japanese leaders were tried before war crimes tribunals, while many of their soldiers were held for long periods in prisoner-of-war camps. Everywhere, post-war reconstruction was slow and painful, but in every country there was a strong desire never to relive the horrors of World War II.

UNITED NATIONS
The United Nations is one of the lasting legacies of the war. Representatives of 26 nations, including the USA, USSR, Britain, and China, met in Washington DC on 1 January 1942. Each agreed not to make peace with the Axis (Italy, Germany, and Japan) without the other UN members. A permanent United Nations organization was established in October 1945, with 51 members.

PREFAB HOUSING
Prefabricated (ready-built) houses were used in Britain to house the thousands of people made homeless by bombing. The steel, later aluminium, and asbestos prefabs came in kit form and took a few days to construct. More than 150,000 prefabs were erected in the 1940s. Although intended as a temporary housing measure, some still survive today.

RUBBLE GANGS
Across Germany, the inhabitants worked to clear up their ruined towns and cities. They emptied bombed buildings, swept roads of rubble and helped in the reconstruction. The work was hard and unpleasant, as they often found decomposing bodies in the cellars and basements of buildings.

Wreck of Hess's Messerschmitt Me110 fighter

CRASH LEADS TO PRISON
On 10 May 1941, Rudolf Hess, deputy leader of the Nazi Party, flew from Germany to Scotland. The plane crash-landed and Hess surrendered, claiming to be seeking peace. Hess was given a life sentence at the Nuremberg trials, and remained in Spandau prison, Berlin, until his death in 1987. The exact circumstances of Hess's flight have never been fully revealed.

WAR CRIMES TRIALS

After the war many leading Nazi and Japanese officials stood trial charged with various war crimes. At Nuremberg, Germany, 1945-6, a trial of 22 leading Nazis was organized by an International Military Tribunal of US, French, Russian, and British judges. Twelve of the 22 defendants were sentenced to death. In Japan, General Tojo was executed in 1948. Further trials, such as this one of Nazi prison camp officers in 1948, continued for many years.

RATIONING CONTINUES

The end of the war did not mean the end of shortages across Europe. Until farming and industry could return to normal production, food and basic essentials remained in desperately short supply. Bread was rationed for the first time in Britain in 1946, and rationing of meat did not end until as late as 1954.

British Ministry of Food ration book for 1949–50

PEACE PARK HIROSHIMA

This memorial stands in Peace Park in Hiroshima. The park is a reminder of the terrible damage that nuclear weapons can inflict upon people anywhere. Since the war, peace campaigners around the world have protested to make sure that the two bombs dropped on Japan would remain the only nuclear weapons ever used in war.

AFFLUENT AMERICA

The USA emerged from the war far stronger and far richer than it had entered it. With the exception of its Pacific islands, no part of the country had been bombed or invaded and its people now entered a time of full employment and rising wages. Many Americans could afford to buy the newly built suburban homes and cars.

Index

Acknowledgements

Dorling Kindersley would like to thank:

Terry Charman, Mark Seaman, Mark Pindelski, Elizabeth Bowers, Neil Young, Christopher Dowling, Nigel Steel, Laurie Milner, Mike Hibberd, Alan Jeffreys, Paul Cornish and the photography archive team at the Imperial War Museum for their help.
Jacket design: Piers Tilbury
Design and editorial assistance: Sheila Collins and Simon Holland
Index: Chris Bernstein
Additional picture research: Samantha Nunn, Marie Osborne and Amanda Russell

The publisher would like to thank the following for their kind permission to reproduce their photographs:
a=above, b=below, c=centre, l-left, r=right, t=top;
Advertising Archives: 51bc, 63clb.

Airbourne Forces Museum, Aldershot: 32-33.
AKG London: 45cra, 51t; German Press Corps 13tc.
The Art Archive: 30cr.
Camera Press: 7br; Imperial War Museum 53tr.
Charles Fraser Smith: 26cra.
Corbis UK Ltd: 33tr, 40c, 59br; Bettmann 54-55b, 61; Carmen Redondo 52-53; David Samuel Robbins 63r; Hulton Deutsch Collections 20cl, 31tr, 53tc, 62c.
D Day Museum, Portsmouth: 54cla.
Eden Camp Modern History Theme Museum, Malton: 22cl, 29tr, 36bl, 60bl, 62cr, 63cl.
HK Melton: 16c, 17cla, 17c, 26bl, 26br, 28crb, 31tl, 31cl.
Hoover Institution: Walter Leschander 28cb.
Hulton Getty: 8cl, 8bl, 10cl, 14cr, 16tt, 17tl, 23tl, 26crb, 38b, 39cl, 39br, 43tc, 56b, 57c, 57br; © AFF/AFS, Amsterdam, The Netherlands 37tr; Alexander Ustinov 60cl; Fox Photos 20bl; Keystone 12tc, 14b, 15tl, 25tc; Keystone Features 28ca, 29b; Reg Speller 36br; US Army

Signal Corps Photograph 53cr.
Imperial War Museum: Dorling Kindersley Picture Library 16br, 26cl, 26c, 26cr, 37tl, 45cr; IWM Photograph Archive (reference numbers in brackets)11cr (ZZZ9182C), 21cr (HU1185), 21tr (HL5181), 22tr (HU635), 23tr (CH1277),24cl (B5501), 34 cr (TR1253), 34bl (D18056), 35bl (IND1492), 40br (IND3468), 41cr (C4989), 44t (RUS2109), 48cl (E14582), 50cr (C494), 56c (BU1292), 56cr (6352).
Kobal Collection: Universal 48cra.
Mary Evans Picture Library: 9br. M.O.D,
Michael Jenner Photography: 6l.
Pattern Room, Nottingham: 47b.
National Cryptological Museum: 31cr.
National Maritime Museum, London: 42-43c.
Novosti: 46cr, 46bl, 47tl, 47cl; 45t.
Oesterreichische Nationalbibliothek: 9tl.
Peter Newark's Pictures: 6cr, 8tl, 11tr, 12-13tr, 13b, 15cra, 17bl, 18c, 19bc, 19br, 22c, 25cl, 26cl, 31br, 32clb, 34tr, 35br, 36tl, 37b, 41b, 47tr, 50b, 51bl, 52bl, 55cr, 58tr, 58-59; Yevgeni Khaldei 57bc.
Popperfoto: 17cra, 29cr, 34br, 35tl.
Public Record Office Picture Library: 26cla,

30crb.
Robert Harding Picture Library: 59tr.
Robert Hunt Library: 22-23b.
Ronald Grant Archive: British Lion Films 12b.
Royal Air Force Museum, Hendon: 26cla.
Royal Signals Museum, Blandford Camp: 55tr.
Topham Picturepoint: 9cl, 29cl, 41cla, 43crb, 48tr, 49tl, 49tr, 50cl, 51br, 52c, 53br, 63tl; Press Association 41tr.
Trh Pictures: 24bl, 32tr, 37tc, 38c, 55tl, 55c; Imperial War Museum 33tc; Leszek Erenfeicht 8-9; National Archives 24-25b, 39t; United Nations 58br; US NA 54tr; US National Archives 42clb.
Weimar Archive: 9cr.

Jacket credits:
Chrysalis Picture Library: front cra.
Hulton Getty: Reg Speller back cla.
Imperial War Museum: front tc, back tc.
Peter Newark's Pictures: front cl, back br, back cra.
Topham Picturepoint: front bl.
Trh Pictures: back crb.

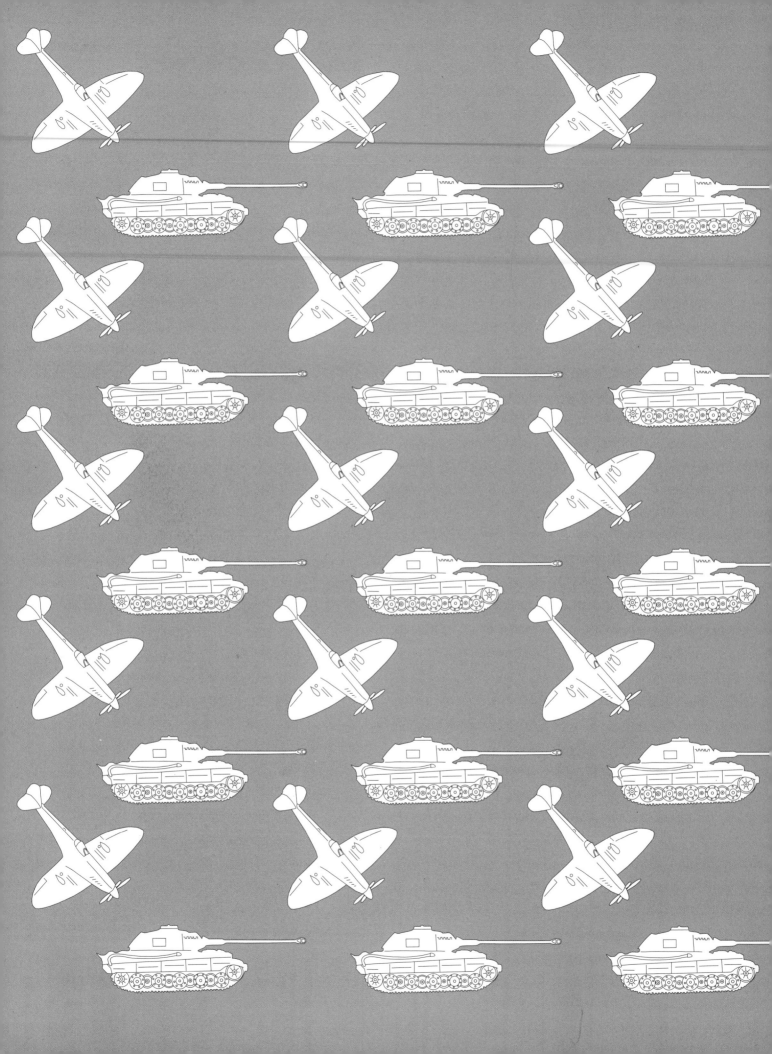